IN THE STUDIO

Heart

IN THE STUDIO

JAKE BROWN

ECW Press

Published by ECW Press
2120 Queen Street East, Suite 200
Toronto, Ontario, Canada M4E 1E2
416.694.3348 / info@ecwpress.com

LIBRARY AND ARCHIVES CANADA CATALOGUING IN PUBLICATION

Brown, Jake
Heart : in the studio / Jake Brown

ISBN-13: 978-1-55022-831-1

1. Heart (Musical group). 2. Rock musicians —
United States — Biography. I. Title.

ML421.H436B87 2008   782.42166'0922   C2007-907100-7

Interior image credits: From the author's collection (© Ann and Nancy Wilson): pages 16, 17, 28, 30, 35, 45, 103;
© Chris Walter: 56, 70, 111, 139, 142; © Hulton Archive/WireImage: 81; © Ron Galella/WireImage: 90;
courtesy Deb Ivester (phoenixheart.org): 98, 118, 128, 135, 173, 178, 188, 190, 210, 212, 218, 238; courtesy Brian
Hawksford: 125, 166, 181, 208; © Sue Ennis: 137; © Ron Nevison: 149; from the Photofeatures Archive: 154; © Jay
Blakesberg: 198; © Andrea Gonzales (the-heart-blog.com): 223, 244, 252; © Marijn Veenhuizen
(www.heartlinker.eu): 232; © WL Meier: 241, 257.
Photo section credits: Pages 1 and 4 – from the author's collection (© Ann and Nancy Wilson); page 2 (top) – ©
Chris Walter; page 2 (bottom) – © Neal Preston/Corbis; page 3 – © Brian Hawksford; pages 5, 6 (top), and 7 –
Andrea Gonzales (the-heart-blog.com); pages 6 (bottom) and 8 – WL Meier.

Special thank you to all the Heart fans who generously contributed
their photos, and time, to *Heart: In the Studio*.

Editor: Crissy Boylan
Cover and Text Design: Tania Craan
Cover photo: © Chris Walter
Typesetting: Mary Bowness
Production: Rachel Brooks
Printing: Thomson-Shore

PRINTED AND BOUND IN THE UNITED STATES

ECW PRESS
ecwpress.com

Dedicated to my late Papa, Armand Thieme, R.I.P.

&

to Jackson Rollin Schuchard, first son of Alex and Lindsay,

born February 2008 . . .

Acknowledgements

First and foremost, I would like to profoundly and sincerely thank Ann and Nancy Wilson for participating in the writing of this book, I have been a lifelong fan of Heart, and it was a true honor that you contributed interviews.

Next, I would like to say another HUGE THANK YOU to Jack David and ECW Press for taking a chance on me, and giving this book a home.

To Sue Ennis, I will spend a long time beyond this page or the publication of this book thanking you for your considerable time interviewing for (and EDITING) your 18-page interview!! As well, thank you for the photos, and for sharing your memories of writing and recording some of our favorite Heart classics!

To Carol Peters, Sue, and everyone else at Peters Management who green-lit and orchestrated the interviews with Heart, my SINCEREST thank yous.

To the many producers who spent HOURS on the phone in initial and follow-up interviews to make this the most complete study of Heart's catalog it could be: Mike Flicker, you have my gratitude for the extensive time you took with me in fleshing out

Heart's unique recording methods; Ron Nevison, as someone who grew up on your productions throughout the 1980s, it was an honor to have your participation in this study; Keith Olsen, it was a true privilege to have your inclusion in this project, thank you; Ritchie Zito, as another producer whose sound I grew up on, it was a great thrill to have your involvement in this project; Brian Foraker, thank you; and finally to Duane Baron for your reflections both on working with Heart and the late John Purdell, R.I.P.

Personal thanks to my parents, James and Christina Brown, for your tireless support of my pursuits; my brother Sgt. Joshua T. Brown, welcome home, December '08!; the Thieme and Brown families; Alex and Lindsay Schuchard — congrats!; Andrew and Sarah McDermott; Chris Ellauri; Sean and Amy Fillinich; Adam Perri; Matt Pietz; Alexandra Federov; Penelope Ellis; Paul and Helen; Tony and Yvonne Rose; Burt and Jan Goldstein, Larry et al @ Big Daddy Music Distribution; Bob, Reed, Tim, and anyone and everyone else who grew up with me, and maybe yourselves on HEART!

Table of Contents

Rock 'n' Roll Suffrage

Saying that men dominated hard rock in the 1970s is an understatement. Rock radio hits routinely and blatantly sexualized women — "Radar Love," "Rock & Roll Hoochie Coo," "Cat Scratch Fever," "Hot Blooded" and "Love Gun" to name a few — and virtually *all* of the bands recording those songs were comprised of men. Testosterone-dominated bands like Black Sabbath, Led Zeppelin, Lynyrd Skynyrd and Aerosmith rose to the heights of rock in the early '70s while a strong female presence had been lacking since the death of Janis Joplin in 1970. Female artists of the time, like Joni Mitchell, Joan Baez and Carly Simon, who wrote topically on women's liberation, were popular in softer, folk and pop-rock genres, but in hard rock, women were largely without a voice for the first half of the decade.

But that void was filled when the debut LP by Seattle-based, hard-rock band Heart, fronted by Ann and Nancy Wilson, took the rock world by storm in 1976, producing two smash singles, "Crazy on You" and "Magic Man." *Dreamboat Annie*'s success would change the face of rock forever as it unabashedly brought the softer side of acoustic rock together with songs that rocked as hard as any of the band's all-male contemporaries. In its review of the ground-breaking album, *Rolling Stone* raved that the band had "successfully challenged the heavy testosterone in hard rock with Ann's keening, Zeppelin-like vocals [that] shift from pop-thrush blandness to piercing shrieks with the stroke of a power chord . . . and [with] Nancy's monster pop-rock riffs."

As the burgeoning format of album-oriented rock poured out of transistor radios across North America, men and women in the ranks of blue and white collar workers paced their work clocks to anthems like "Magic Man," and celebrated quitting time at happy hours with the flirtatious frenzy of "Crazy on You." The second wave of feminism was in full force; with the Supreme Court's decision in *Roe v. Wade* in 1973, women's liberation was abuzz in American culture like a hot guitar amplifier. And in rock arenas, Ann and Nancy Wilson represented the *only* mainstream, female-fronted rock 'n' roll band.

Heart's success proved women could rock as hard as men — at the same time that women were fighting for recognition that they competed equally in the workplace. This theme would remain relevant to the band throughout the 1970s and beyond. As the band rose through the charts, the chauvinist ranks of the recording industry — promoters, managers and record label executives — all pushed for image over substance to capitalize on the Wilson sisters' sex appeal. Their struggle would inspire smash hits like "Barracuda," all while the sisters firmly stuck to their guns and stayed true to themselves for over three decades through ups and downs as they adapted to the changing music industry.

The legacy of Heart is at its core in the songwriting and performances captured in the studio on their twelve LPs. Here, album by album and in their own words, the Wilson sisters, band members, songwriters and producers tell their story of creating the music of Heart.

CHAPTER 1

The Wilson Sisters' Very Musical Childhood and Teenage Years

Rock 'n' roll in the 1970s was the eccentric offspring of the pop-culturally stormy 1960s, when rock 'n' roll and the record business were both in an experimental period. New bands shaped musical genres — Bob Dylan with folk-rock, Jimi Hendrix and The Doors with blues-based psychedelic rock, Velvet Underground with the roots of punk rock, or in the case of The Beatles and The Rolling Stones, and to a slightly lesser degree, The Who, bands redefined rock 'n' roll itself. As the 1970s rock scene took form, groups continued to define new stylistic niches of their own — Black Sabbath and Led Zeppelin with heavy metal; Pink Floyd and Genesis with art-rock; the Ramones, The Stooges, the New York Dolls, and the Sex Pistols for mainstream punk rock; Aerosmith and Kiss for hard rock;

Ann Wilson in the infancy of what
would become a lifelong love of dogs
Bruce Springsteen for blue-collar
rock; Alice Cooper and David Bowie
for theatrical and conceptual glam
rock; Fleetwood Mac with pop rock; and for women in hard
rock: Heart.

The two frontwomen of Heart, Ann and Nancy Wilson, rose
to the heights of rock 'n' roll as early as the mid-'70s, but they
started life in a simple Seattle home always filled with music. In
a 1980 cover story on the Wilson sisters, *Rolling Stone* described
the girls' childhood and home: "Ann and Nancy grew up on
166th Avenue in Bellevue, a middle-class suburb of Seattle . . . in
a two-story house [where] . . . the well worn spot on the recre-
ation-room floor was where [Ann] and her sister practiced the
guitar. . . . Inside Ann's old bedroom, across a narrow hall, the
talk turns to the sisters' teenage years: the acid trips on Ringo
Starr's birthday; the stoned joyrides; the pusher who'd throw lids
of grass through Ann's bedroom window; the hours spent

behind closed doors in those little rooms, writing poetry, playing records, daydreaming." In the article, Ann Wilson described a stable childhood in which "while we were doing all this stuff, we felt really unusual. . . . But we were pretty normal for the time we grew up in. What we experienced was going on in suburbs all over the country. We weren't that different. . . . There are a thousand places that look just like this. You see them when you go on the road."

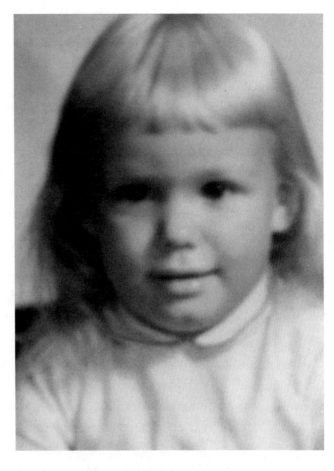

Nancy Wilson at age three

Speaking to the girls' parents, *Rolling Stone* gleaned that "the Wilsons are an old military family, going back several generations. John Wilson [father to Ann and Nancy] was a colonel in the marines who settled in Seattle after retiring and taught English at Sammamish High School. While Nancy and Ann were growing up, they lived in Southern California and Taiwan with their older sister, Lynn (now in Oregon with her four children)." Living in Seattle, Washington, the Wilson sisters grew up in the same hometown as rock legend Jimi Hendrix, as well as blues and jazz legends Ray Charles and Quincy Jones, all of whom influenced the then-forming musical sensibilities of Ann and Nancy.

Music was the voice that interpreted the social changes that

> **'It was such a rich time in music culture. . . . A revolution to be exact.'**

Ann and Nancy witnessed as the civil rights movement gained momentum across the nation. Nancy described her record collection as reflective of the issues of the time, a collection that contained "many influences other than The Beatles, including Simon and Garfunkel; Led Zeppelin; Elton John; Crosby, Stills, Nash and Young; Joni Mitchell; Ray Charles; Aretha Franklin; The Who; The Moody Blues; Jackson Browne and so very many more. It was such a rich time in music culture to be learning the trade! A revolution to be exact."

It helped that the sisters came from a musically open home; Nancy remembered that "growing up we always had a good sound system in the living room, and our parents would really turn it up. They loved the classics, opera, Ray Charles, Harry Belafonte, Aretha, Peggy Lee and Judy Garland as well as experimental electronic modern composers. There was no lack of variety. They became big Beatles fans too by the late '60s." Ann Wilson, in a 1980 interview, recalled her parents listening to "Porgy and Bess, Puccini, Gershwin . . . the ones that were the most accessible opera . . . *Madame Butterfly* . . . and then as we got older I remember my mom played a lot of Ray Charles. . . . I used to love Judy Garland a lot; I thought she was really something . . . and then later on my older sister got into Little Richard. . . . [I also listened to] Aretha Franklin, and other stuff. I got into Robert Plant a lot, I was into McCartney — I learned how to kinda say words and stuff by listening to his songs."

Revealing her family's musical lineage, Nancy explained that her parents "both had sung in choirs and our mom played concert piano locally as a college student. I remember watching her feet pump the pedals while lying under the baby grand as she practiced pieces from Rachmaninoff and Beethoven as well as ragtime greats. As a family we spent plenty of time singing with grandparents, aunts and uncles who all liked to pull out ukuleles and do funny old pub songs and Hawaiian songs that we still know to this day; we still play ukuleles and our kids are next in line." Ann added that their parents "were music lovers themselves, so they had an open attitude about music. . . . My mom didn't like it much when I bought my first record, which was *Baby Love* by The Supremes. She went, 'You were supposed to buy your school lunch with that [money]. What are you gonna eat for the next week?!'"

So liberal was the girls' upbringing that, according to their mother Lou, "we smoked pot with our kids and did other things we never dreamed of doing. I marched in a peace march with three daughters and a grandson on my shoulders. . . . At the same time our children were going through the '60s, so were John and I. We left a world of phoniness and suburban values and became active in social issues. . . . We had incredible friends, and an incredible support system based around the Congregational Church. It's a very liberal church, with young ministers." Captivated by the vibrant times, the Wilson girls shared another near-religious experience with other would-be rock stars who were children in the early 1960s: listening to The Beatles. Nancy recalled that "right from the beginning, as soon as we saw The Beatles play on the Ed Sullivan variety show . . . Ann and I started begging and pleading for guitars. I was eight and Ann was twelve when we started learning our first chords from the trusty Mel Bay chord book. With the basic cords under our belt, we would spin Beatles records and learn every song."

More than just a strong musical influence, The Beatles helped the Wilson sisters meet a classmate who would become a lifelong friend. Sue Ennis recalled that "it was the beginning of junior year in high school, and The Beatles had just played Seattle the week before. I had just moved to Seattle; I really didn't know anybody but I was a huge Beatles fan. And they had just played August 25, 1966, at the Coliseum in Seattle, and it was just before their final show at Candlestick Park [in San Francisco]. So my dad showed me this picture in the morning paper, and said, 'Oh, there's a girl from your high school who won The Beatles contest.' And so I looked, and there was a picture of this girl, Ann Wilson, holding a little movie camera she'd won for an essay about 'What The Beatles Mean to Teenagers.' It turned out she was in my German class, but I didn't really know her. So the following Monday, I sat down behind her in class, and started singing the most obscure Beatles song off the *Revolver* album — which had come out recently — just to see if she knew the deep cuts. It was 'Love You To,' a George Harrison song, and she whipped around, and said, 'Oh, do you have *Revolver*?'

"And we started talking, and couldn't stop talking, and right off, recognized in each other a serious, serious fan-ship. It was more than just 'They're cute guys,' but that The Beatles had been an object of serious scholarship, study and dedication on both of our parts. We both recognized a mutual expertise that we felt set us apart. I would say Ann was inspired by their singing, but was *blown away* by the way they put chords together. She had already gotten pretty good on the guitar a couple years earlier when she'd had mononucleosis, and didn't go to school for three months. Her mom bought her a little cheap acoustic guitar, just to give her something to do, and she went after it in a big way. She learned a bunch of chords, and had a wonderful ear. And so when the Beatles came along it was her mission to learn and figure out as many songs as possible. By the way, her favorite Beatle was and will always be forever more Paul McCartney. There was definitely the 'cute guy' aspect, but it was more than that. I think it was his melodies, and that she understood that he was a melodic genius. She was in awe of the musicality that The Beatles had."

Once The Beatles had captured their creative attention, Nancy remembered that the sisters "started writing songs right away. Not that any of the first songs we wrote were much good, but by imitating many of the hit songs off records and the radio, we got a solid sense of song structure." To learn the guitar chords and changes between them, Nancy credited "the vari-speed feature on the turntable, which allowed us to play songs at half tempo . . . extremely handy when changing to the new chord took some doing." As the sisters imitated their favorite band's hit records, they also imitated their moves, practicing rock poses before the vanity mirror. Ann recalled, "When we were kids . . . [we'd] take brooms, tennis rackets," pretending they were guitars. Nancy once told a journalist that "we just had to be as much like The Beatles as we possibly could, learn every song, wear jeans with bare feet and pea coats, walk through the stores with black Beatles boots and go look at The Beatles' magazines and things like that."

Before developing their own artistic sense of self, the sisters first found inspiration in other bands, not just in the musicality of The Beatles, but in the raw power of Led Zeppelin. Nancy credited Led Zeppelin with providing the girls their first glimmer of a creative vision that would eventually become Heart. "I saw Led Zeppelin live for the first time when I was 13. I remember sitting there with Ann, and we were blushing 'cause they were so raw. It was disturbing yet alluring. We were already doing music together, mainly because of The Beatles. But when we got into Zeppelin, it really helped to form our identity. These guys were not just playing straight power chords. . . . What Jimmy Page did was pretty inspiring for guitar players. He married a lot of acoustic elements into hard rock. The kind of chords he used were very left of center, with a lot of dissonance — I absorbed that like a sponge. It's all over the music I write, always."

As the girls blossomed into songwriters in their teenage years in the mid-to-late 1960s, their compositions were tried out for their first live audiences. Nancy recalled, "While we were still living at home writing songs, we'd always audition them for anyone who'd listen. Lucky for us there was always a supportive friendly atmosphere even if the learning curve was still curving." The support system the girls had growing up was invaluable to their future success; Ann summarized it with a quote from their mother: "Mom would always say . . . that it doesn't matter what you do, as long as you do your best, and you're happy. I don't think she thought we would end up in a rock band."

Childhood friend Ennis explained that "music was always playing in their house. Their dad was a school teacher, and he'd come home at three o'clock and put on music — whether it was the radio or an LP. [He'd] walk around the house and correct papers, whistling and singing along. So it was a very relaxed — compared to my family at least — kind of a dreamy atmosphere. The parents were there of course, but they didn't really meddle, and we just spent hours up in the bedroom, playing records, away from them. So once we'd lock into this music haven we inhabited together, we were inseparable."

Even as children, Ann and Nancy had an ever-present sisterly and creative closeness. As Ennis remembered, "Ann would say, 'Call me up,' and I'd call her to talk about The Beatles. And I'd find that her sister Nancy was always there in the background, laughing and jumping around, and Ann would barely pay attention to me because they were laughing so much. So I really wanted to meet this little sister. I had my own beloved sister, but we were *never* like Ann and Nancy; they were just spiritual twins. Nancy was 12 years old and Ann was 16, and at first, I couldn't understand why Ann would be hanging around with a 12-year-old. Until I met her, and then realized that she was brilliant and funny and not a kid. My friendship with Nancy started later than Ann, but it was almost as instantaneous, because we instantly fell in together over this passion for music."

Ennis recalled, "When I met Nancy, at age 12, they already had a little group going called The Viewpoints, that was based around complex harmonies. They had always had *big* harmony singing in their family growing up. Their earliest songs were definitely influenced by putting similar chord progressions to The Beatles' together. I don't think they had their eye on being a rock band back then though. I think they wanted to be just a musical group with great harmonies. In addition to The Beatles, they were inspired by The Left Banke — 'Walk Away Renee' and 'Pretty Ballerina' — and even The Association. Those types of softer sounds. Their harmony singing had started when they were kids traveling in the car with their family, and singing all the time. Especially with their sister Lynn, too. They were doing musicals, and one of their greatest harmony songs ever was 'If I Loved You,' the famous song from *Carousel*. The three of them had a natural ear and blend, those extraordinary 'blood harmonies' that families have. So by the time I came into the picture, they were really good. The first time I met Nancy over at their house, she and Ann got their guitars out and started playing, and they were mind-blowingly good. I had a guitar, and they taught me chords, and we started to sort of jam off other people's songs. You'd be singing a Beatles song, and then keep playing the chords, and develop something new. Then I remember fairly early on, I hadn't seen them for a couple days, and went over to visit. Ann and Nance said, 'We wrote two songs last night. You want to hear them?' One song was called 'Through Eyes of Glass,' which Ann later recorded for the Topaz label. But even back then upon first listen, I thought it was incredible. I couldn't believe the professional level it was on for beginning songwriters. I could hear a little Beatles influence but it seemed original too. I think this was the first song they seriously wrote, where they said, 'Let's write a real song,' instead of jokey songs. Because we'd written a lot of songs prior with crazy lyrics, but when I heard that song, I knew they were even more talented than I already thought."

While the stereotypical teenage girl spends all her time socializing, Ennis recalled that Ann and Nancy preferred to spend every waking moment of their time writing and singing together. "When I first met [Ann], she was the most single-minded person I'd ever met, including all the adults in my life. She just wanted to write poems and short stories, draw — she was a pretty good artist — and sing. That was it. She didn't want to read books, or go to movies much. She had no interest in going outside. In high school, she was definitely not a social butterfly. Ann was a super-outcast at school; she went her own way, and the first time I saw her, she was like no other girl in our high school. She had her own style: she carried her notebook and her books sort of under her arm like a guy, rather than the proper way up around her chest to look cute and girly. I remember I invited her to my sixteenth birthday party, and because I was a pretty good student I had some smart girls in my circle, and I thought, 'Oh, this is great, we can all get along. I can introduce them to my odd, weird, fantastic artist friend'; it was oil and water. Ann would stay by herself, while I was talking to some of the other girls, and she'd come over, and sort of whisper, 'Hey, come over here, let's talk about The Beatles.' She just didn't want other people. She is an extraordinary being. My theory is that she was dropped on the earth from another planet, just because she was out of step with what ordinary teenagers do. I was intensely drawn to her because of that. And sometimes along the way I felt like I needed to protect her, give her little hints about certain things to show her how other people operated. She was just her own, odd, fantastically gifted person.

"Nancy was much less shy than Ann growing up. She had a couple of friends in high school who became really close, and who also played a little guitar. She also had some boys after her, and she wasn't particularly interested in that, but she had a couple of dates I think. The guys were just crazy for her, but she was more into the world of music and guitars." Offering a fly-on-the-wall view of the Wilson sisters' formative, rock-star-in-training years, Ennis remembered, "One night, when their parents were gone, we were playing some record really, really loud in their family room where we used to hang out. I think it might have been 'Brown Sugar' by the Stones, a song we all loved so much. We were dancing hard. I got winded, and threw myself down on the couch, and when

'Ann was a super-outcast at school; she went her own way'

I looked up I saw the two of them dancing together, just rocking out and totally happy, these gorgeous girls. And I thought, 'Man, these sisters are amazingly charismatic. They're riveting. I wonder if I could ever share the vision I'm having right now with the world? Because I'm the only person who gets to see how magical these people are right now.' So when they went on to take their magic up onstage in front of thousands of people, I was amazed. It was like it was already destined way back in their living room that night. I got to be their first fan! We marvel sometimes at how close we've stayed over the years. The most fun is when it's just the three of us. We have a long-standing tradition — as old as our friendship — of getting together on Christmas Eve, carving out a couple hours and exchanging joke presents, writing fake cards and comedy letters, to entertain each other. It's similar to what we've brought into the studio over the years with *Connie*. Lucky for us, that part of our teenage friendship is still there."

These formative years of Ann and Nancy Wilson — learning by imitating their rock-star mentors and hammering out their first original compositions — soon led to the sisters' debut musical forays out of the living room and onto the stage.

CHAPTER 2

Heart's First Musical Beats

The Early 1970s

As the 1970s began, the Washington region's — and specifically Seattle's — local, live scene was a well-kept secret, with Seattle rock historian Jim Page describing the music scene as invisible: "Way back in those days of broken cars and low rent. The early '70s. It was a sidewalk town back then, with lots of buses and tree-lined back streets. And music. Lots of music. You never would have heard about it if you weren't there. There was no music press and you couldn't get famous unless you left. But it was magic. . . . I got here in '71 and broke right into it. The last folk club closed and I started carving out a reality in the any-thing-goes world of the already happening night life. And the day time life too — the campus and the streets. But the rock clubs were happening at night and the music was good. Bands

Ann with one of her first bands post–high school

like Butter Fat and The Doily Brothers. Mojo Hand and Lance Romance."

Among these bar bands cutting their teeth in early 1970s Seattle was Heart, a band formed more than a decade earlier in Vancouver, British Columbia, by Roger and Mike Fisher and bassist Steve Fossen. Back in 1963, the guys originally called the band "Army" but by the start of the '70s, they had renamed themselves "White Heart" before settling finally, and simply, on "Heart." In 1968 following Ann's graduation from Sammamish High School, she moved from Seattle to Vancouver, after she "met Roger [Fisher] and Steve [Fossen], and we formed a group. I was the 'chick singer' — ha! One night we had a gig playing in Bellingham, which is a college town up north. Mike [Fisher] was in Canada then, times being what they

> 'The "tough chick" thing
>
> was all a front.'

were. . . . Before I knew Mike, when he lived here, he went through this 'acid priest' phase. Got into Eastern religion. At one point, he was running around in military fatigues, with his head shaved, giving acid to people. Anyway, we played this club in Bellingham, and Mike sneaked down to see his little brother's new band. He'd heard his brother say there was this chick in the group, and when he walked into rehearsal, there she was, sitting on the dance floor wearing old jeans with this big ciggie hanging out of her mouth, a glass of wine, trying to learn the words to this Janis Joplin song, 'Move Over.' Yeah, man. A tough chick, y'know? Mike kinda went, 'God, who's that?' and stuck around that night. He drank a pitcher of beer, and we started to get to know each other. It was one of those deals where things go *gonnngggg*! He asked me to go up to Canada with him. But I was too scared. The 'tough chick' thing was all a front. I thought he just wanted to, uh, make it or something. But eventually, I just had to move to Canada. I just kind of came with him. It lasted nine years."

Continuing with her recollection of the band's early days in Vancouver, Ann explained, "It was really hard times. There I was, I'd followed this man to Canada. We all lived in this one room — this is the story everybody in the band hates now — and ate brown rice. Steve and Roger were married then, and they had their wives there, and Steve had a child. I had to learn to be one of the hens. It just drove me crazy! This middle-class princess from Bellevue had to wash her hair in cold water and be the cook of the house." Establishing their popularity as a bar band by mostly playing cover songs, Ann recalled a set list and schedule

heart

Early promotional poster from the band's club days in Vancouver, B.C.

that included material like "'Pacific Gas' and 'Electric,' 'Proud Mary,' 'Susie-Q,' 'Jumpin' Jack Flash' or something else by the Stones . . . 'Honky Tonk Woman.' We used to do a lot of stuff by Zeppelin, tons of Zeppelin stuff. We did 'The Rover,' 'Cashmere,' 'Battle of Evermore,' 'Rock & Roll,' of course, 'Communication Breakdown,' and 'Whole Lotta Love.' . . . Usually in the States it was four sets [a night, but] in Canada it was five."

Sue Ennis, who kept in close contact with both Ann and Nancy post–high school graduation, recalled these early days with all three of them separated as hard for the sisters. "Ann always felt even more at home with Nancy on stage beside her. This didn't happen till much later. Once we graduated, I headed off to college down in Salem, Oregon, and in some ways it was excruciating for me. I was living alone in the freshman dorm, and was kind of lost, because I'd been living in this amazing artistic bubble with my best friends. So it was wrenching for me to be separated from them, almost worse than leaving my family. We'd see each other at Christmas, and spend the whole two-week break jamming and playing guitars, but our paths diverged then, even though we kept in the closest contact. We wrote letters almost every day, but they were not about what was happening in our 'real' lives; they were about trying to keep our world alive. They were funny, insider jokes, little cartoons, little missives that said, 'Our little world is still breathing.'

'That's where she was great and grand, and at ease, and not an outcast.'

"At this point, Ann was playing in bar bands around town, was really starting to develop her voice. She was out five nights a week singing, and just getting really, really good. I don't think those were particularly prolific years in terms of songwriting. I think this was Ann's education time, getting out on stage and singing, singing, singing. Ann had been a straight-A student in junior high school, then when music came along, she derailed in school. I also think by the time she graduated high school, her parents realized that she didn't have aspirations to go to a four-year university. She just wanted to do music. I think that being up on stage every night, learning to connect with the audience, is where she developed her social side. At first it was a little awkward for her, because she'd be incredible singing and then step up to the mic, and just not know what to say. Over time though, she developed that skill and became a charming emcee, because that was her platform. That's where she was great and grand, and at ease, and not an outcast. In fact, she was *always* a star onstage. That's where she discovered another life where she could be sought after and popular, and at ease.

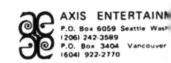

AXIS ENTERTAINM
P.O. Box 6059 Seattle Wash
(206) 242-3589
P.O. Box 3404 Vancouver
(604) 922-2770

The stage is a place where she truly shines and thrives. After Ann had moved up to Vancouver, Nance really missed performing with her. Nancy really saw herself as a singer/songwriter in those days, while she was separated from Ann. So Nance played in coffee houses, and got a pretty good set together. Some Seals and Crofts, some Elton John, and Joni Mitchell. She was fearless; it was just a girl with her guitar, singing and playing in front of many audiences. But both she and Ann had a natural confidence on stage that was like, 'Here I am,' a truly fearless confidence.

"Nancy was in college in Oregon — maybe following in my footsteps a little bit — at a place called Pacific University in Forest Grove. And she had school work to do, but she found a coffee house in the little town of Forest Grove, and made the guy give her a couple nights a week gigging. She seemed to need to supplement college with that, just as her own way to keep moving forward as a musician. I saw Nance live many times back then and I was her biggest and most thrilled fan. Sometimes she would come to Salem from Portland State and stay the weekends with me, and we'd play guitars all the time. I also was really into literature at that time, and was studying German lit. So we read *Metamorphosis* by Kafka, and [also the Russian novel] *Crime and Punishment* by Dostoevsky. We were discovering world lit, besides some of the Hemingway-type short stories we'd been brought up on in high school. I was the English major, so I was telling her what to read, and she would read them, and we'd have great talks. I remember when she discovered J.D. Salinger, she found 'her' author. She first read *Catcher in the Rye*, and then went and got all of his titles, and read them over and over. *Frannie and Zooey* was one of her favorites, to the point that she actually named two of her dogs Zooey. So I would say Salinger's world was the heart of everything she loved for a few years."

Mike Flicker, founder and head producer of Mushroom Studios, who would go on to produce the band's first five albums, initially heard of Heart from an assistant engineer. "When I first became aware of Heart . . . Nancy Wilson wasn't in

'. . . you just knew Ann was going to be a star.'

it; it was only Ann at that time. And they were playing locally in Vancouver and didn't have a record deal yet. And one of the engineers who worked for me at Mushroom, Rolf Henneman, was a fan of theirs and was after me for a long time to check them out. So when I finally went to see them live, I *loved* Ann. I thought she was excellent: her attitude and tone and power. But the rest of the band didn't impress me at all. And they had a couple of original tunes, which also didn't impress me. So I, basically, on first listen passed, and told Rolf, 'If anything happens with the band, keep me abreast.'"

It was Mushroom's in-house arranger, assistant engineer and childhood friend of the producer, Howard Leese, who would actually record Heart's first demo. Leese recalls that "my first work with Heart was as a producer. Actually, it was funny — they came in to do their demo, and Mike wasn't there that day, so I produced the first demo with Rolf engineering. They were playing in the clubs in Vancouver, and Rolf saw them and brought them to Mike. I don't think I'd seen them until we started working together. . . . The big thing was Ann's voice. Nancy wasn't even a member at the time when I produced their first demo. They didn't start recording the first album until a year later. When you went to see them in a club, before Nancy, you just knew Ann was going to be a star. Her voice was ridiculous. Even though they were doing covers, you saw her singing better than the real guy. They were real ambitious. . . . The demo was good, but it wasn't original stuff. It was an Elton John song of '60 Years On,' and a medley of some of their club covers, so we could tell there was talent there, and you could hear Ann's voice was astonishing. But you could tell the band still had a ways to go, and needed to write some originals. So the word at that time was 'We like your stuff, but you need to have some originals, so come back when you do.' So a little bit less than a year later, they came back and had most of the first album written."

The catalyst for the band's creative progress came primarily from Nancy Wilson's decision to leave college to join the band. Ann recalled, "Nancy was flirting with joining the band on acoustic and vocals, an element that I felt would kick us into the stratosphere. Was I right?" Sue Ennis was present on the day Ann made the history-changing proposal to her sister Nancy: "I remember one day when Nance and I were still in Oregon in school, I was housesitting for a professor of mine out in this really cool little rural area. Ann slipped away from Vancouver for a weekend, we picked her up at the airport, and the three of us

Outtakes from a '70s photo shoot with Ann

went out to stay at this house. And I remember the big song of that weekend was 'Sailing the Wind' by Loggins and Messina, and we played it over and over and over. We hung out, played guitars, stayed up all night and cracked each other up. It was a fantastic reunion. We were all so happy to be back in our world together, especially in a house where we were free to make as much noise as we

'I really, really want you to join the band. It's time.'

wanted. I remember one afternoon that will be etched in my brain forever. It was October, and the leaves were turning, there was a warmth in the air, but the shadows were cool. We were standing outside, and Ann turned to Nance out of the blue and gave her speech: 'I really, really want you to join the band. It's time. The musical direction we're going in is cool, but we need your input. We need your acoustic guitar. This band is not going to be complete to me until you're a part of it. You gotta consider coming up.'

"At first I remember Nance was reluctant. She was a die-hard folky, acoustic singer-songwriter, and she told Ann, 'I don't want to spend my days doing "Rock & Roll Hoochie Coo."' This was a simple-minded bar song that everybody covered. Then she said, 'I need for there to be a softer side to the band. That's what I would bring, and this is a band I would be interested in because it would have more than one dimension.' Now, the guys in the band really just wanted to rock, so Ann made this pledge to Nancy: 'I promise you this is what it will be. If you will come, we will make this happen. We will insist on adding this dimension to the band. We will add great, soulful songs to our set.'"

According to Ann, fortunes changed for the band when "Nancy finally came up. We were so crazy to play together. And when she did, I started to return to myself, 'cause I was getting real far away, really starting to become 'a chick.'" Heart returned to their hard rock roots, as engineer and future lead guitarist Howard Leese remembered, "I had gone to see them live, and Nancy had joined the band by this point, and they were doing a lot of Led Zeppelin material — two whole sets, two 45-minute Zeppelin medleys — which was really the thing that changed Ann from being a '60s-style, folk-chick style singer to being a real kick-ass, front woman, rock 'n' roll lead singer because she was doing Robert Plant. The guys in the band were huge Zeppelin fans, Roger Fisher

specifically as I remember. So I think they, as a band, just naturally went to that heavier style once they realized Ann could really sing that stuff. It was just a good fit."

Nancy, for her part, once recalled to a journalist, "In the early years . . . the band was all hard rock. Ann really wanted [diversity] because her own tastes were broader than just what they were doing. . . . It was an intentional thing bringing me into the band for the more melodic side of it, and more acoustic capabilities, which can be brought back to the hard music too. You take the acoustic thing, then you blend it with the heavy handed, sledgehammer drums and you've got Heart. We have both tendencies, and have managed not to kick them out. . . . [Our early days in the clubs] were really important to our growth because we learned how to play there. You know, all those five-hour-a-night gigs that we did all week long, every week. We really got the stamina. We learned how to play tight, in almost any circumstances, whether or not there were brawls or whether there's only two people there."

Producer Mike Flicker remembered that "months later, Howard came back to me and said Ann's sister Nancy was coming up to join the band. And that intrigued me, because it would be two girls in the band. So I basically authorized them to do a demo based on just hearing that news, without even hearing Nancy, who had been down in Oregon going to school. Funny enough, working with me at that time as Mushroom's in-house arranger was Howard Leese. So Howard and Rolf went in and did a demo with them before I got involved. So one of the tunes, a song called 'How Deep It Goes,' which Ann had written, caught my attention out of the batch, and so then I went back and listened to the band live, and it was a whole different band. They went from being just a stock rock 'n' roll cover band to Nancy's addition of the acoustic guitar and harmonizing vocals with Ann. It just added a different flavor that made them original enough for me to think they had something special. I thought they were definitely stars."

Once Nancy had joined the band, the nature of Heart changed. Sue Ennis recalled, "She and Ann just went in and hijacked the group. The sisters were a force and they were united. Remember, there were a lot of hot-headed guys in the band, who just wanted to play Deep Purple and Zeppelin covers, and they certainly did that well. But Ann and Nancy came in at that point and told them what it was going to be. Ann had also gone to school on Aretha Franklin and Dusty Springfield, and she is just an incredible blues singer, so that was a big yearning *she* had — to tap into that style of singing. At the time Ann approached Nancy about joining Heart, I think she was feeling hemmed in by the 'It's got to rock' kind of philosophy in the band. From that point on, throughout the band's history, there has been a struggle between Ann and Nancy and the band guys' big push to rock hard, all the way along. And Ann and Nance loved to rock, but they would always push back, insisting on more thoughtful, more melodic songs. And that began when Nancy joined the group."

Signing the band to a production deal with Mushroom Studio's in-house label, Mushroom Records, the band entered the studio with producer Mike Flicker at the start of 1975 to begin a year-and-a-half-long recording odyssey that would result in the birth of *Dreamboat Annie*. Describing some of the history and design specifics of the band's recording home for the first three albums of their career, Flicker explained, "What they didn't have in Vancouver at that time was a large room. So I ended up finding a studio that somebody had built, and I just fell in love with the room because they hadn't done it out of necessity, but I felt acoustically it was wonderful because it was built on the side of a hill. So about three quarters of the room was underground, just in the shape of the way they had dug out from the hill. And they had built it out of a cinderblock construction, which I just think is wonderful for sound. It was a large room with 29-foot ceilings, and what had happened was the guy who had built the studio was an older guy in the recording business in Vancouver, who had just had a heart attack and wanted to retire. So he had just built this place and the building was brand new. All he had in there was this beautiful room that had a four-track tape recorder and a four-bus board; it was basically a P.O.S. So I went to look for my favorite sound, and was just always a fanatic of tubes, and one of my favorite experiences was recording at Western Studios [now Ocean Way Studios] in L.A. because they had a completely tube board. And that was the time when everyone was going solid-state and getting rid of their tubes, and of course, everyone needed larger consoles now because things were moving from 8 to 16 and 24 tracks at that time. And this particular console at Western was originally built as a two-channel stereo console, and then had been modified by Western, which was a division of United Audio, so by the time I saw it, it had been upgraded to a four-bus board. And I just loved the sound of it; I think it was the warmth and the punch of tubes, and just the whole kind of transparent sound. And I was in the middle of watching the transition — when I started out every console was a tube console, and as the solid-state consoles were coming in, I wasn't liking what I was hearing.

> 'I just loved the sound of it . . . just the whole kind of transparent sound.'

"What happened was basically I bought the tube console from Western because they were upgrading to a solid state one, and had it shipped up to Vancouver and retrofitted by adding some line amps to it to a 16-bus console. It was a cumbersome console to work on, because every kind of EQ and everything was all outboard gear. I was very fond at the time of outboard gear like LA-2AS and LA-3AS, and I had a lot of old tube gear. So it was a lot of tube compressors, but I also had 1176s, and some of the better solid-state compression and things of that nature, but used a lot of passive EQ, which maintained the integrity of the tube. When I purchased the console, I purchased just a shit-load of UA-mated passive graphic equalizers, where we had 8-ban and 12-ban graphic equalizers. The biggest issue with a tube console was heat, because you have to have a huge air conditioner because it really heats up a room, really hot. So we got a big air conditioner. The studio had one really good built-in vocal ISO-booth, rather large, and right off the control room.

"So once I had Mushroom Studios set up, locally at the time I was the only record producer in Vancouver who had hit records. And when I got to town, I discovered there wasn't a good engineer, so by default, I became an engineer as well as a record producer. Through working with local bands I developed that craft, but I had brought with me more knowledge of what I had seen happen rather than done as an engineer. Being that I ran the studio, and was a partner, what we used to [do since we were] doing our own production [was] spend all the time we needed because we didn't have the budgetary constraints, so everything was an experiment. So I would hear something on the radio, go out buy the record, put it on and listen, then go into the studio and try to get that. I'd sit around with people who wanted to do demos and would play for free, and I'd play, and tweak, and try to figure out how they had gotten that sound. That approach worked perfectly for producing Heart, where things were kind of backwards as far as what usually happens. In a certain sense, the first album was their studio days — where if you take The Beatles or someone like that, their first five or six albums were rushed out there, and they didn't really get a chance to take their time and work in the studio till their latter days after *Sgt. Pepper*, whereas Heart got that opportunity right out of the gate."

CHAPTER 3

The Songwriting Craft of Ann and Nancy Wilson

Any artistic recognition Ann and Nancy Wilson have ever sought — be it on an album or in performance — has always been rooted in their songwriting. While the Wilson sisters arguably had a leg up with their undeniable good looks — especially among the tens of thousands of male fans who flocked to their concerts — there was an equal number of female fans and record buyers who identified first and foremost with the messages in the sisters' songwriting. Whether writing about teenage hearts aching or being carefree in love, female sexuality or its commercial exploitation, Ann and Nancy knew their audience as well as they knew themselves. More importantly, they knew how to reach that audience in songs that, much like the sisters' looks and voices, were too beautiful to soon forget.

> '**Even when Heart's rocking,**
> **there's always an acoustic**
> **at the center.**'

The seeds of that musical beauty were planted years earlier when the girls first began writing together as teenagers, with Nancy Wilson recalling that "at the beginning [songwriting] was always as a twosome. Ann would most often have the lyrics or at least a title and concept, and I would contribute most of the guitar changes." Ann explained that the acoustic guitar was such a key part of their songwriting roots because "of course that's what Nancy and I learned on. That's our main core instrument. Even when Heart's rocking, there's always an acoustic at the center of it and I think acoustic guitars are almost holy myself. They're just the coolest instruments in the world. You can do so much with them, they have so much character, the way they're made. They're beautiful to look at, to hold in your hand and they have great voices."

The other set of magical voices that accompanied the guitars, and truly brought any Heart song to life, was the sibling tonality between Ann and Nancy — the combination that produced the beautiful harmony lines, which have become a staple of many Heart classics over the years. The pair's creative process is at its core natural and simple enough that, as explained by Ann, "you can sit around the living room and do it. It's very low tech, you don't have to haul around a bunch of gear necessarily, although they make these acoustic amps, they're so small and cool. And it's really a chance to sing, to sing in harmony and it's much more human. Get together, sort of a hootenanny-type feeling. That's what I love about it." Nancy, for her part, explained, "There is a sibling blend with harmony singing that's genetic [with Ann and me]. . . . It's like ESP. The breathing, vowels, releases and phrasing come together like magic. Singing harmony is always one of the biggest thrills for me."

While sibling tonality was one reliable presence in Heart's songwriting, the germ of a song's lyrics came from a variety of inspirations. According to Nancy, "We've never used any one stock process with song lyrics. Often it's just a musical groove, or a title idea, or another beloved song will get us inspired. There's so much to relate about living in the world. Even though there are really no original themes or stories to tell, it's more about the way you tell the story."

While keeping an open mind, Ann conceded that one area the sisters have always tried to avoid "are 'victim songs.' It's been done and done to death. So we usually try to stick to more personal-universal themes. I'm sure we will always find some new way to write about love until the end. 'The big L' — now there's a theme!" On the duo's lyric-writing methodology, Ann elaborated that "someone will come in with the idea, in some cases all the way there, or we'll take the idea off the way the groove feels.

> ## 'Nothing is ever etched in stone until it's done.'

Sometimes somebody reaches out into their life and writes about that autobiographically or sometimes as in the song, you know, the oldest story in the world, you write what it's like to watch the news these days."

Offering a historical context to Ann and Nancy's more-than-30-year songwriting partnership, lifelong friend Sue Ennis clarified their roles: "It's commonly thought that Nance comes up with the music, and Ann with lyrics, and I would say those are their natural inclinations. But back then, whenever Ann jotted down some lyrics, she always showed them to Nance, and Nance would give her two cents, or would say, 'That's cool.' Ann would always take Nancy's suggestions and incorporate them; it really was a partnership. It was the same thing for coming up with chord progressions, and music writing. Each person already knew what her strengths were, and it just naturally fell into place. I would say Ann was more active in the music side of the writing in those days. They'd work out the chords together, and then Nance would go and just practice it. The thing about Nance was that she had this incredible discipline about practicing the guitar that I don't think Ann had. Ann had a natural gift for hearing things and melodies, but little Nance quickly took over as the more powerful guitarist, because she worked at it all the time. Nance and I wrote a couple of songs together early on when Ann was gone somewhere, but they were more joke songs. We loved to write stupid lyrics, but it was really for our entertainment, like the funniest game you could ever play. All the time we were messing around this way, we were learning how to fashion song structure."

Continuing with her firsthand recollection of Ann's development as a lyricist, Ennis recalled, "When I met the Wilsons, Ann had already written three novels. They were contained in these large three-ring notebooks, and she typed them out on her ancient typewriter. Her novels were based on English musicians — clearly like The Beatles — and they were these deeply felt romantic fantasies about music, girlfriends and boyfriends. They were very chaste. No sex anywhere to be found. Each one was a dreamy, teenage girl projection of what love could be. Ann is a visual writer, so they were very wonderfully detailed with happy endings. And these were like 300-page novels, so I think a lot of our songs grew out of that. We were going to write love songs. She had had a lot of experience describing love and the heartbreaks, but very little experience with boys. But still I loved her books; they were escapist, fantastic romance novels. So that's the source of the early songs."

Using "Dreamboat Annie" as an example of the sisters' craft in action, Nancy recalled "that was one of our first, first songs. We wrote it at our parents' house, at the coffee table in the living room. It was finished in about a half hour, the quickest we've ever written a song together. We were trying to be the Beach Boys, I think." Elaborating, Ann remembered that originally she "had written a poem. Not the lyrics, but the poem that appears on the album sleeve about a little, little wooden ship and a person thinking of herself as a wooden ship. This was another way I was thinking of myself at the time. Leaving home, going out to find your romantic fortune and yourself. All the stuff you have to find when you're 20."

As the principal architect of the musical side of a Wilson sisters' song, Nancy explained her process of inspiration, "As a player, I've always got all kinds of melodies and music floating around in my head. Sometimes, I have to stop whatever I'm doing and make a quick recording, singing or playing these scraps of music to compile and uncover later, or just scribble down some word ideas. Many times one of these riffs or tunes will follow me around for days or weeks until I can capture it or sort of wrangle it to the ground. Though, just picking up a

> 'We strive for live band takes in the same room all together. . . . First instincts.'

guitar or sitting down at the piano brings a new journey on the spot. Different voices of different instruments will lead you to places you didn't know you were going. The mandolin and mandocello have been favorites lately. Different instruments inform you of what they want to say and you come to find you're just there to translate and get it down." At this point in the songwriting process, as Ann once explained, the sisters come together to turn these pieces into a whole: "[Nancy will] maybe have a musical idea for a groove. She works with a lot of unusual tunings. So maybe she'll have a tuning that she really wants to get into or maybe I will have words or a title. We'll just get together and just throw it all in a pot and start working with it like clay until we have a song. Once we have a song then we treat it like a song and start tuning it up."

Once the song has entered the demo stage, Nancy quipped that there have been times over the years of writing hits together where "in the process of translating song demos to full band recorded productions, the beautiful germ of the song [got] lost. 'Beating the demo' is always tough, and rarely succeeds. It's a rather painful topic!" Even when a demo has progressed from pre-production to proper recording, with the group satisfied the song's basic musical components have been fleshed out, Nancy and the band still consider that song in its writing stages, reasoning that "mapping out the final shapes of a melody is something that can still happen up to the final vocal, although we keep all the vocals in case the early ones had the magic. Nothing is ever etched in stone until it's done. Some new solo, melody, sound or arrangement idea can spring up too. It's all about serving what feels natural and good, and avoiding what feels tedious or straining. We strive for live band takes in the same room all together. Fewer overdubs. First instincts." Those instincts have produced countless classic rock hits over more than two decades, beginning with the band's debut LP, *Dreamboat Annie*, of whose material *Rolling Stone* would correctly conclude "proved that . . . good songs can go a long way commercially."

CHAPTER 4

Dreamboat Annie

1976

Rolling Stone, at the end of its October 1976 review of Heart's debut LP, *Dreamboat Annie*, concluded that "the success of Heart ... should point the way to still more acceptance of women rock singers in a field still very dominated by men." Hailing the band as "the left-field commercial success of the year," and praising lead singer Ann Wilson's voice as "strong, flexible and emotionally captivating," the magazine further concluded that "her phrasing is as confident as Helen Reddy's, her timbre seductive as Christine McVie's, and her scalding hard-rock attack not unlike Robert Plant's; it is her performance which holds together the album's sharply defined ... themes of supernatural love and sexual hysteria." Taking the rock world by storm, the phenomenon of a female-fronted hard rock band that could musically

> '. . . all the songs that were written for that album are . . . from real life.'

hold its own alongside the most popular male hard rock counterparts was instantaneous, in part because the band had no female competitors. The success of *Dreamboat Annie* among hard rock fans made Heart contemporaries of pop-friendly guitar-rock arena acts like Boston, Rush and Styx, as well as harder rock super groups like Led Zeppelin (who had been a strong musical influence on the band).

Heart's songwriting skill ensured that the public's ears would be as equally tuned in to the group's songs as their eyes already were to their image, an issue Heart would struggle with for the next three decades. The band had a dual fan base that included the requisite legions of male fans attracted to the band's arena rock riffs and the Wilsons' irresistible sexuality, as well as millions of teenage female rock fans who could relate to the lyrical narratives in ways the male contingent mostly did not. With the explosive rise of the women's liberation movement in the first half of the 1970s, and with the release of Fleetwood Mac's *Rumours* LP still three years away, hits like "Crazy on You" and "Magic Man" became the first anthems for a new generation of female rock fans with the themes in Ann and Nancy's songs ringing true. Against an equally electric musical backdrop, Heart explored themes of love, lust, innocence lost, jealousy and sexual liberation from a female perspective instead of from the traditional chauvinist slant of rock 'n' roll. As a result, Heart's female fans were freed to rock out as hard as they ever had to male-fronted bands, but with a fresh sense of identity. As Ann Wilson put it, "all the songs that were written for that album are . . . all from real life. Very sweet and very innocent [songs] . . . about going out into the world." And that realism enabled listeners to connect in a visceral way to the music.

Though *Dreamboat Annie*'s success seemed overnight to many, the record took a year and a half to create, and was among the most conceptually and sonically labored-over debuts of hard rock's most pivotal decade. As Nancy Wilson recalled about the album's genesis in general terms, "*Dreamboat Annie* was being recorded off and on during a long period while Heart was still playing cabarets, clubs and grad party dances all over Canada. We were writing the whole time too, so it came together gradually, which was more a blessing than a curse." Ann remembered, "*Dreamboat Annie* was recorded in 1975 to '76 in Vancouver, B.C., at Can Base studio. We had managed to get a tiny indie label, Mushroom Records, to record an album using staff producer Mike Flicker. No advance, just some penniless, American, transplanted club musicians living in a band house, who got a lucky little break. The album took a while to record because we were touring at the same time."

In a unique situation, Heart's sound as a band was evolving at the same time their debut studio album was being recorded. Producer Mike Flicker explained that, from the outset, "when we went in to do recording, I think we were maybe all a little wide-eyed, but I didn't predict there would be any problem except regarding changes in the band line-up, because of personal problems. And I had told them prior to going in that 'I would love to record you girls, but I'm not convinced about your band.' And it was a double-edged sword, because I really think Ann and Nancy felt the same. But they were young, there were loyalties, and there were relationships too, because Ann's boyfriend's brother, Roger Fisher, was the guitar player, and so it became

> 'I would love to record you girls, but I'm not convinced about your band.'

'. . . never overstated or trying too hard to show off his huge talents. [Howard's] sound was all his own.'

quite clear that that was the only non-negotiable situation. So by the time we went in to record, Howard Leese was also contributing musically as a second guitar player."

Howard Leese had started out as one of the album's engineers, but his addition to the band rounded out their sound. As Nancy explained, "When we asked Howard Leese to be in the band, he was already a producer at Can Base when we were recording *Dreamboat Annie*. He'd done some touring, and was reluctant at first. But when he started seeing us live and then played parts on the album, mostly keyboards at first, I think he saw we weren't just messing around. He became the second lead player and later the main lead guitar. I always loved his restrained, soulful, bluesy choice of notes and phrasing, never overstated or trying too hard to show off his huge talents. His sound was all his own, always like a rock during his many albums and tours with us." Before formally joining the band, Leese was involved with the making of *Dreamboat Annie* as an unofficial band member: "Originally my main job on that record was going to be to write the string arrangements and conduct the orchestra, which I did, but I ended up playing on it more than I'd expected to, because they were a band already — in a live sense."

Leese was first brought in by Mike Flicker as a go-to session guy because "[Heart] had spent a lot of time recording, and it was slow-going, so they brought me in to help that along. It was mainly Roger Fisher who would spend a lot of time trying to figure out what he was going to do, and Mike would get frustrated with the experimental nature of that kind of stuff. Roger had great energy, and he was very creative, he would come up with stuff that no one else would think of, very original ideas. Between he and Nancy [they were going together at the time], the thing that was cool about that is they were really trying to learn together and would teach each other stuff, and were taking lessons together. So they, as a couple, were together all the time, and really seemed to be the quintessential *musos comaraderie*, always working on stuff, thinking about stuff, making things up, writing different things, playing guitars and mandolins, so I thought they were a really strong musical force. As a writer, he was very important to the early band, but his focus as far as coming up with a strong part, he played a little differently every time, and would wander around in the studio trying all these crazy ideas. And when they worked, it was fantastic, but 80 percent of the time it doesn't work. That gets tough on the producer, but Roger was a very creative guy. He has a lot of creative energy, and real unusual ideas, definitely has his own style, but he's not a schooled musician. He plays by ear, and doesn't really know the theory of why things work and why they aren't gonna work, so I think that became frustrating to producers. So [Flicker] would bring me in after a while to just knock it out — do some overdubs and guitar stuff because I was faster as a session player. Also, in the studio, there were five different drummers on the first record, so he was a little bit frustrated, and so he brought me in to speed things along after it was about halfway done."

Flicker, for his own part, felt that Leese's involvement as a band member was pivotal to completing both the album and Heart as a musical entity. "They asked Howard Leese to formally join the band, which was great for me because by the time of Heart, Howard and I had been working together for 15 years, and we used to just do things by looking at each other. Howard's greatest strengths were first that he was a rounded musician. He did the string arrangements, and played guitar and keyboards, so he had an understanding of musical theory and could help

them. So it began as a musical respect, and grew in time into a camaraderie that brought him as a full-time member into the band. He was the only one who had any kind of recording experience, and I think that helped them to have that anchor. I think that's what he always was, a musical anchor, and they could relate to him, and there was a certain amount . . . Because Ann and Nancy had no, let's say, formal musical background in music theory — to have someone who had that background and someone they could relate to who had a good ear, gave them a certain comfort factor. There was a trust there, and typically, anyone who I've ever worked with who is not a trained musician, usually has an Achilles heel about that. They'll always be defensive about that kind of stuff, you constantly hear, 'I don't know a third from a fifth.' People get defensive about that, and Howard helped to make up that slack in the band."

Leese, who would become a co-lead guitarist by the completion of the album's recording, explained that his position instrumentally in the band was "funny because I had replaced the keyboard player originally. They had an organ player, who ended up joining Bryan Adams' band for many years. So as a keyboardist originally, I had to learn like five sets of cover songs, and the one thing Ann said to me was 'You can do whatever you want, but no Hammond B3. You can do whatever you want, but no organ.' She apparently didn't like the keyboard player very much or the sound of the organ, she was tired of it. So when I joined, I played some guitar, but did a lot of the keyboard stuff for the first few weeks. I ended up doing six or seven weeks of club dates, then we started playing concerts. All I had to do was forget the other four sets. Heart always did one original set, but before that we'd do Zeppelin sets, and medley sets, then the biggest part of the night was doing the original set. So when we made it to the concert set, all we had to do was play originals, which meant I was playing a lot more guitar, based off the large amount of that I'd been doing off stage in the studio." In describing the on-stage dynamic between himself and fellow guitarists Roger Fisher and Nancy Wilson, Leese explained that "live, between Nancy, Roger, and [me] as the guitar players in the band, Nancy generally played the acoustic, and Roger and I did the electrics and we'd split the leads up pretty much 50/50. He was originally the lead guitar player, but then I played a lot of the solos on the record, and on things like 'Crazy on You,' that had a duet solo. We recorded that live together after we came up with it in the studio, which was fun because it was a little more spontaneous. Nancy played a little bit of electric. 'White Lightning and Wine' was an electric riff she came up with and played on, but she preferred acoustic; it's always her first choice."

In terms of capturing the trio on tape in the studio, Flicker remembered using Leese as an anchor, "Roger, in terms of the strengths he brought to the band, was wild abandonment. So if Howard was in the pocket, Roger was bouncing off the walls, and Nancy was somewhere in the middle. When I mixed their guitars, it was, what is the emphasis? It almost felt like Roger could come up with parts that were significant, in the early days. His playing of the riff of 'Crazy on You' was my inspiration for the whole structure of the song, as far as from a radio *single* point of view. We used words like *hook* back then, and when I heard that riff, I said, 'This is the hook for the song.' And it was his riff on 'Barracuda' that was the hook on that song. And then live, I think he was a bigger asset than he was in the studio, because he was so off the wall in terms of his energy. The guitar blends were created as we'd go, and one of the things that I used to like to do a lot — and was one of the things that got Howard and Nancy at an early stage working together — was to record acoustic guitars at the same time. A lot of their stuff was two-part acoustic guitar things, so Howard would play one and Nancy would play the other. They fed off each other's instincts. Howard was more structured, and Nancy was more unstructured and free, a little more raw, and I think that helped a lot.

Either one — Howard could get technically off where he could get cold, Nancy sometimes left alone could get too wild in abandon. They had kind of a yin and a yang that worked well together. In the early days, anything that was

dual guitars, Howard wrote and taught to Roger Fisher. Nancy was more there for rhythm and groove."

Regarding his preferences mic-wise for capturing the album's wide-ranging electric-acoustic guitar sound, Flicker detailed, "For guitar and bass, I used to use a combination. With the bass, again, because I loved the sound of the tubes, I used a direct sound that went through tube pre-amps, then had this little ampeg 15-inch single speaker that I loved the sound of, and had that as the mic sound. And it would kind of combine the two of them to get the sound I wanted. Mostly for that, I loved the RA20 on that, and it was the bass sound you heard on *Dreamboat Annie* and most of the Heart records I produced. For guitars, I was really a Marshall guy, and had my own 100-watt stack that I really liked, and had tweaked out. I always liked a close and a far mic with a condenser close — a Buyer M69 that had this really nice 3 K and 300 cycle hum to it. And I would then use a condenser mic from a distance, which was a 414. For acoustic guitar recording, I typically would use condenser mics — my C61 console mic, an AKG and a C12A. I had some guitars that I liked including a D12, as well as, for Heart, Nancy had this wonderful custom-made acoustic guitar that was made for her by somebody. I loved the sound of that guitar."

Even with Leese solidly on board, a major logistical dilemma Heart had to manage during the album's recording was their ever-changing line-up of drummers. Ann noted, "A few musicians outside the band contributed to the making of the album, mostly

'. . . we found ourselves in drummer hell.'

drummers, including Dave Wilson [no relation] and Duris Maxwell. Mike Flicker also played some drums, as well as a conga player from the local drum shop whose name now escapes me, but who made a big difference on 'Magic Man.'" Expanding even more candidly on the subject, sister Nancy remembered that "we found ourselves in drummer hell, trying to find the guy who would hopefully go forward all the way with us, so there were a few different drummers on the album and the dynamics of choosing only one guy was rather intense." From a production perspective, ranging from stylistic differences to their effect on maintaining a consistent micing dynamic for the album's drum sound, Flicker recalled a technical juggling act, "Dave Wilson was their drummer at the time, and we were supposed to do six tracks. Of those, the only thing I could get out of him was 'Magic Man.' Then Kat Hendricks came in and played on 'Crazy on You,' and a few others. I found my favorite bass drum mics, and would go between the RE-20 and the D12, and I liked AKG dynamic mics, and my favorite snare-drum mic was using a C61, which was an old condenser mic. Aside from being just an exceptional microphone, it had all these wonderful capsules that you could screw on, and had one that was this really tight cardio pattern that was really good for the snare. And these million screw-on pads that allowed you to really pad the microphone prior to its own internal amplifier, and would allow you to use a good condenser microphone without overloading on the snare. And I'd go from using that sometimes on the top, and sometimes would use it on the bottom with a Shure 56 or 57 on top. It just depended on the situation and the sound. And I'd simultaneously mic the bottom and the top of the snare that way.

"For overhead mics, I used a C12A, and what I always liked to do was use an unmatched pair set of mics. I know everyone always liked to use matched sets at the time. But I would use an unmatched pair set, because one of the other things I liked was the mid-range crack that I would get out of an old U87 Neumann, so I would put that above the snare on the left side, and the C12A just always has this extraordinary top and bottom that would pick up from the floor toms and the cymbals on the right-hand side. Also, I pretty much had my drum kit set up with that mic set-up, and had a band's drummer play my kit — which was basically a mutt, in that I had an old Rogers bass drum that I really liked, and a couple Ludwig snares, and the toms were a combination of Camco and Pearl. The range of the mics to the drum set would often depend on the drummer and the size of the drummer, and the throw and how he played. For *Dreamboat Annie*, I only had one side of the kick drum miced, and pretty much the traditional sound of that time. Basically, what happened was the drummer who ended up on about three cuts on *Dreamboat Annie* — Michael Derosier — ended up being their drummer. And he came from the John Bonham school of drumming, and strictly was a double-headed kind of guy."

The band fluctuated back and forth between live touring stints and in-studio sessions, and the recording atmosphere very much mirrored the spontaneity of the band's live shows with Flicker's live-off-the-floor tracking approach to capturing the band on tape. As the producer explained, "Back in those days, we were working on 16 tracks, so there wasn't a lot of room for many, many takes. For the recording of all of the songs on *Dreamboat Annie*, they always tracked live in the studio as a band. Most of the songs on the album were all done in the studio first, and then live, so they were really morphing as a band during the studio process." Adding to the producer's challenges navigating the fluid nature of the sessions was the fact that the band's material was being written *as* they recorded. Throwing out the time-honored recording norm of writing the album's songs during pre-production, Ann Wilson explained that "back then we didn't do any pre-produc-

> ‘They always tracked live
> in the studio as a band.’

tion; we just recorded the songs as they were written — good thing we felt like writing — and Mike Flicker helped get them into shape during recording.”

Also untraditional was how the concept for *Dreamboat Annie* evolved, as Flicker explained, “Back then, we were making a record for Canada, and had our own label, Mushroom Records, so we recorded the song ‘How Deep It Goes,’ released it as a single, and it had moderate success. Then we recorded ‘Magic Man,’ and that had big success, so after that we said, ‘It’s time to do a follow-up single and an album.’ That was pretty much proper marketing in Canada at that time. You couldn’t really market an album without a couple successful singles. So they were playing me songs, and one day played me ‘Dreamboat Annie,’ and I said, ‘I don’t only love this song, I love it as a concept for an album.’ And so I threw that back at them, and then we talked about the way it would work in an album. So they said, ‘Conceptually, we hear it this way,’ and played it. And also, I said, ‘I think it would sound great as kind of a perky, country-ish song, with the banjo and whatnot. Then to wrap up the album, let’s reprise it with an orchestral version.’ So with that in mind, we basically recorded all three at the same time. We recorded them as three separate songs, but that album title and theme came out of a collaboration of ideas.”

Coming up with the individual songs that would make up Heart’s debut album, Ann and Nancy “usually had in mind what they were going to write about before they wrote about it,” according to *Dreamboat Annie*’s producer. “The two of them would sit down, talk about it, and that’s what they’d write. Our process for developing songs always was Ann and Nancy would come with a song, and have something worked out — a basic theory — and I’d say, ‘Well, how about if we double a chorus here, and how about let’s repeat this bridge here.’ It would always be taking the pieces they had, and restructuring them. Ann was a pretty quick lyricist, so if we were in the studio, and I suggested a new lyrical part was needed, she could whip something out pretty quickly. A lot of times, at the very beginning, they'd play me songs that weren't even finished yet where they were just looking for input. They were just really quick on that, and what I even noticed throughout their career is whenever I would talk to them about structure, or work on a song in the aspect of structure, that the next time they would write, they were such quick learners that those concepts were now incorporated and adapted to everything. So though they'd come in with demos, our approach to writing back then was to treat it as a collaboration, such that the first album, every time Ann and Nancy would write a song — in the rawest sense, where sometimes it was just a verse and a chorus — they'd call me up, and we'd sit down and they'd play it, usually on an acoustic guitar with vocals. Nancy usually came with the music, and Ann not only with lyrics but also with melodic ideas. Sometimes they had pre-worked out their harmonies. So what we used to do when we were arranging for the album, most of the time, I would play drums and we sat in the studio with the two girls, Howard and I, and the bass player they had at the time. He had a really great attitude, and ended up staying in the live version of the band, but the problem I had was I didn't feel his playing was up to par at the time for studio recording. But he sat in on the demos."

Howard Leese agreed that "[Ann and Nancy's] songwriting was really good, and getting better quickly, early on there. Nancy was an amazing acoustic guitar player. She has hands stronger than most men; she has very, very strong hands, and can really play the acoustic guitar. She's a great writer — writes most of the music. When she and Ann get together to write, Nancy generally has some chords, and Ann would have a vocal melody. It moves around a little bit, but generally Nancy would come up with the germ of a musical idea. Nancy would have melodies too, she knows more about musical structure — as far as chords — because she's a good instrumentalist, so they would both have melodic ideas, and would work in the lyrics together as well. Early on, they both contributed equally to the lyrics. Ann may have had a little bit more to do with that."

As far as the album's lush instrumentation on acoustic tracks like "How Deep It Goes" and "Dreamboat Annie," Leese explained that he "wrote those parts with Rob Netes, my keyboard player. I would have the basic track, and the strings were the last thing to go on, so in writing the parts, I would take the song home and sit at the piano and figure out where I wanted the strings to enter, which parts of the song they were going to be in. Then try to write the general parts, and once I had an idea of what the parts were going to be, I would voice the orchestra a certain way. So then you write the bass, the high and medium violins, and Ann and Nancy's voices are just such a beautiful sound that they made the string parts stand out that much more. I think that's another reason why those first five records still stand out today is because they have real, live string orchestras. This was before we really had good enough keyboard technology to do an effective string-sounding thing. The main overdubbing were the guitar solos and the orchestra, and that's the Vancouver Symphony we brought in to do that. There wasn't much synthesizer at all except for my Moog on there. Writing for strings was a lot of fun because the orchestra musicians could play anything, so I used basically the same technique as you would for classical music, and applied it to a rock band. Regarding Heart's general song arrangements, the material itself was a bit unusual — it wasn't the usual verse, chorus, bridge, verse, chorus kind of pop song format. Some of the songs were a little longer form and a little bit different, especially later on as we got into it and got a little more artsy with it. The band's ideas were good, they just needed to focus in and refine it into something that would translate to the listener." Ann told a rock journalist years later that Leese's orchestral additions brought "an honesty, a genuineness, as well as something fresh! Most of those instruments are very old-fashioned, and acoustic, and they really mix well with electric instruments. They make an unusual textural sound."

Reflecting on *Dreamboat Annie* from inception to live birth in the studio, Ann noted, "Nancy and I wrote all the songs except 'Sing Child Sing,' the chords and riffs of which are a band composition . . . 'art' by committee. When it was finished, we looked back amazed at what we'd done, because there had been no real road map. It was just a bunch of songs and a lot of gumption. It was nothing like anything that was being played on the radio. We most certainly weren't sexy disco chicks or leather-wearing Suzi Quatros who might kick your face out. It was something else. I never dreamed they would eventually dig it in Detroit . . . but they did." Fleshing out Ann and Nancy Wilson's demos for songs like "Magic Man" and "Crazy on You" was crucial to creating the smash hits they became. Flicker recalled that with "Crazy on You," while the sisters had come in with a finished demo, "conceptually I had something different in mind. We approached it differently, to where conceptually I always had in mind that the verse and chorus were coming from a totally different place. So I had Ann sing all the verses first, so I always felt the verses and the chorus were two different songs in a certain way. And I always wanted to feel like it was coming from two different places, and they actually overlap. Ann's still finishing the choruses when she comes into the verses. Also, the first time we put it together with the band, when we got to the out section, Roger Fisher played the riff, and that was the first time I'd heard that. They'd written the song, and the first time I heard it with the band with that riff, I just loved it. And we sat down in rehearsal and restructured the entire song around the riff. Nancy had written that riff and played it for Roger on the electric guitar, and we created the beat for the song in the studio. Ann and

Nancy had come up with the rhythm, and then just sort of knowing Kat's style as a drummer, that's why I chose him for that song. And he picked up on that rhythm and threw it into the shuffle on his hi-hat, and put that into the groove.

"On 'Magic Man,' it was more like we took one part and expanded on it, and got different grooves into it. We did various takes that we all liked, and then I'd comp together different parts. We didn't have a real length in [mind], and I think each time it was a different length. I think they jammed it out a little more live, and we had a three-minute radio edit of 'Magic Man,' and I would go in and work on those things, and then Ann and Nancy would approve it. The album-length version ended up being 5 minutes and 35 seconds. When I edited for radio, I was cutting out repetition, trying to keep attention going all the time, and keeping new stuff happening and progressing, and not allowing the song to stagnate. And you're also focusing on radio at the time — I would do something different in 1976 than I would in 1980. The girls understood that game as well."

A key step in the recording process was capturing the sisters' lead vocals and harmony vocal blend on tape, which Flicker recalled was seamless because of their natural talent as recording artists. "In recording Heart vocally, the girls were totally easy in transitioning from the stage to the recording booth. There was no mic-shy; they transitioned into the studio without any problem, which can often be a problem with artists who are totally green to recording. It's very different in nature from performing live. They were a pretty good collaboration in part for that reason, I think because we were arranging the songs together, it always was that way."

Aware that he had helped to discover a rock voice that had the potential to define a generation of women rockers to come, guitarist and co-producer Howard Leese felt after witnessing Ann tracking in the studio that "without a doubt, the band's greatest strength was Ann Wilson's voice. There's nothing like it

— she's the greatest white rock female singer in history. She's the very best there is, and no one is even close to her. All we had to do was not screw it up: we had to have good songs, and let her sing. All through the whole thing, my main job

was to provide a good showcase for her voice. The greatest strength was her voice, number one." Flicker recalled that Ann's vocal talents translated well in the recording booth, making her a pro as a studio vocalist. "Ann was an excellent performer, so once she got warmed up, you just started taping and keeping. I always recorded warm-ups from the get-go, and sometimes the first, second, third take, there's [usable] stuff there. With Ann, it didn't take long, and at that point in time, we never had the luxury of keeping one or two takes at a time because of track availability. So once I'd got what I called my master take, then I would just start punching in, fixing any little flaws. Ann usually got a performance in one take, and it was usually 60 to 90 percent of the song, and then it was a matter of fixing this or that."

Expanding into the technical specifics and norms to tracking Ann Wilson, Flicker "used to record Ann's voice, all treated with effects, totally with repeats and everything on it. A vocal microphone that I found and kept through my entire career recording with Ann, to where every vocal I recorded was recorded on one mic, a very early U87. When I was recording Ann for the first time, I was actually in the market to buy a new microphone, so I had a rep in Vancouver who repped AKG, Buyer, and Neumann, and he came and brought every vocal mic they had. So we lined them up in the studio, and I had Ann come and sing one day, just playing with sound, and she sang into every microphone they had, and one microphone just grabbed me over the others, and I bought that microphone personally and kept it with me for a long time. As far as effects I put on Ann, I had this disc delay system — it would kind of be like an echoplex, but it was made in Germany, and instead of being tape, it was a magnetic disc with movable heads. And so you could get the exact delay that you'd want, and then it had its own regeneration feedback loop, so you could get as many repeats as you want. I used that till it broke, around the end of *Dreamboat Annie*. What I liked about it was the degradation of the high end, you'd be lucky by the time you got to the slap if there was anything above 5 K, and the further out you got, the worse it got. So it was kind of like the old seven-and-a-half IPS slowed down tape-delay kind of thing. Then MXR came out with this thing called MXR DDL, and it was a horrible effects box that I loved, that did the same thing. Again, this was in the '70s, and technically when you got to 500 milliseconds there was no frequency response, so to me it sounded like when you'd be in a stadium, and hearing things coming off a wall. But it worked relative to Ann's voice. The first time I used that second effect was on 'Barracuda,' and throughout the recording of *Magazine* and *Little Queen*."

Of the working relationship between the producer and singer Ann Wilson, Sue Ennis noted, "Mike Flicker was the first studio professional to really understand and value Ann's gift as a singer. This was back in the Mushroom days, and I remember hanging for hours in the studio observing what great, personal touch he had with Ann, knowing how to coax great performances out of her. He had the skills to really connect with her. She respected him, and he understood that when Ann and Nancy came into the studio, you don't just snap right to work. (It probably made him want to slit his throat at times.) But part of their process was getting comfortable at first. You hang out and visit for a while. And their dogs are going to come along. That was just part of the deal. Mike was able to be patient and put up with lots of time that wasn't necessarily focused, while the clock was ticking. I think that they developed kind of an effortless relationship with him over the years. He never pushed too hard, and somehow he understood the approach to take. Some people thrive on that, 'Challenge me and I'll give you something better,' and that was *not* Ann."

Once Ann's leads were

'Throughout history, most of the greatest vocal blends are siblings.'

tracked, the next step was tracking Nancy's harmonies, an easy task given what Flicker described as the sisters' natural sibling tonality, such that "with Nancy, the best thing that she did was she's a great harmony singer to Ann — their voices blend. Throughout history, most of the greatest vocal blends are siblings. There's something about the genetic thing, when people who sing harmony are related. So she harmonizes perfectly with Ann. This was a sisters/partners team who'd been singing together since they were five years old. If you look at further credits on *Dreamboat Annie*, you'll see I brought in their sister Lynn because the three of them together was crazy, in terms of how much that sibling tonality was right there." That beautiful tonality was nurtured from their childhood, as Nancy detailed, "As a young family, we always harmonized on road trips and family gatherings. Aunts, uncles, grandparents and the lot. With our third sister Lynn we learned Everly Brothers, Beach Boys and many old standards. We all sang in choirs and chimed in around campfires. It's a lost art in the family these days I'm afraid!"

Even with that family history, nailing those harmonies is no easy task as the album's producer explained: "When I recorded Nancy, it was usually after I'd get a master track of Ann's lead, then Nancy would come in and do her harmonies, or at the same time. A lot of times, Ann would harmonize to her own vocal with Nancy, and sometimes they'd be together. The cool thing about it is Ann never sings the same way twice. Ann would just sing it however she felt it, and then Nancy would have to go in

and learn the phrasing exactly and do the harmony. So her job was a lot harder. Ann would just go in there and blow, and then Nancy would have to go in and do a tight harmony to Ann's vocal. So that's a hard job. She's great at singing with Ann.

As naturally close as their vocal tonality, the sisters were tied at the hip during vocal sessions, so much so that Flicker recalled, "throughout the entire recording of the first album, I can't remember tracking a vocal with Ann without Nancy by my side at the console. Ann would usually ask for Nancy's opinion when she finished a vocal take. I think Ann felt better knowing Nancy approved. The thing about working with them was, right off the bat, they were — just as people — reasonable people. There were never big egos. If Ann would do something, and I said, 'I think you can do that better,' there was never a problem. And I think it was a mutual respect thing, because if she got a take that I really liked, and she came back in and listened, and said, 'I think I can do this part better,' I'd then say, 'Well, go back and do it.' So I think it comes down to if you have that mutual understanding and respect, it just works that way."

By the time principal tracking was completed, many of the mixing decisions for *Dreamboat Annie* were also completed. According to Flicker, "When I mixed *Dreamboat Annie*, I liked working with the end in mind, and because of the limitations of the gear we had available at the time, and 16 tracks, I was always doing final steps as we'd go. I'd always take great lengths at making my monitor mix something that was a representation of where I was going with the mix, to the extent of 90 percent of all the delay, reverbs, etcetera, that were on vocals and lead guitars. Most of those decisions were made when we were recording. Mixing to me wasn't a big production, where all of a sudden you'd hear things that weren't there before, or that there'd be some crazy things. Even when we were recording the title track, 'Dreamboat Annie,' I'd bring in the ocean effects while we were recording it. It wasn't like we did that at the end of the process, all those things were

'Ann felt better knowing Nancy approved.'

developing as the production was developing." In terms of how involved Ann and Nancy chose to be in the mixing process, Flicker recalled, "On *Dreamboat Annie*, and most of the Heart records I made, Ann and Nancy would come around for the mixing sessions, but their concept of mixing, at first, but in general, mixing was like watching the paint dry. Later on they got a little bit more interested, but usually they'd like to hear something that was more of a finished product, and then comment on it. I think they weren't that concerned because of my production style, where there was never a surprise when the mix came. For myself, I always took great lengths of making monitor mixes that were representative of where I was going."

For Flicker's studio production partner Howard Leese, from a technical vantage point, his favorite thing about that debut album is "that the record still sounds good today. People still ask me how we did that. I think one of the main reasons was that the board that we had was a tube mixing console, which had big transformers and big tubes in the board, which makes everything warm. Tubes make things sound warm and human, and makes the drums and vocals, in particular, just sound bigger and more present. That board came out of Muscle Shoals, Alabama. There were two of them, and Al Green got one, we got the other. It was an old tube board, which you won't find anymore anywhere. The other thing was we used big two-inch tape, and for effects all we had was a real echo chamber, an actual room that you'd send a signal in with a microphone and a speaker. And we had a thing called an EMT plate, which was a plate suspended in the air for reverb. So my point is there wasn't that much you could do to mess it up. Today, there are all kinds of processing gear, where you run your signal through this and through that, and by the time it gets to the end, it's dead. So the main reason

the record sounded so good was it was unadulterated; it was very pure and very basic. Everyone played at the same time, there was very little overdubbing; it's really how we sounded."

By the time of *Dreamboat Annie*'s release, the band's sound and final line-up were firmly established. In Nancy's words, "As a band we really solidified our own character by the end of the *Dreamboat Annie* sessions. A lot of styles and poses that we offered up in clubs were stripped off for the all original, new Heart that felt most like us to us." Ann agreed with her sister's assessment, "the DBA sessions served to transform the lineup into what it was until 1980. This was not a 'concept' album, but it is tied together by the 'Dreamboat Annie' theme. Altogether, the intention was definitely there." Upon completion and release on February 14, 1976, *Rolling Stone* hailed the album as having an "intensity seldom found" and praised "the haunting title theme, an acoustic folk fragment that is developed recurrently throughout the album.... The most commercially successful Heart songs ... graft heavy-metal musicianship to emotional, image-laden lyrics. This unlikely combination is held together by Ann's powerful, three-octave soprano. She can belt and screech the hardest rock tune, then slide through every delicate nuance of tender folk ballad."

The first of several legacy-shaping albums he would produce with the band, Flicker still holds the band's debut album closest to heart: "Looking back on *Dreamboat Annie*, it's my favorite because it was approached by everybody with no expectations, and all anybody was interested in doing was making the best music and the best record for themselves. It's consistently my favorite Heart record, first because of the songs, second because of the performance, and finally, the production. And I would say that's the only album where I felt all three of them were at the same level." The album would go on to multi-platinum status, and establish the band as an overnight arena and AOR-radio staple whose sound, style and influence would be woven into rock's broader musical fabric for a quarter century to come.

CHAPTER 5

Little Queen
and Magazine

1977

Though Heart may have taken their maiden voyage with *Dreamboat Annie*, a short year later as they entered the studio to begin work on their sophomore album, they were already far greater than *Little Queens* among rock fans. Standing out in the otherwise male-dominated arena of rock, Heart employed a groundbreaking strategy which put the personal and social issues that the sisters were so passionate about in the forefront of a provocative rock 'n' roll narrative. The Wilson sisters backed that narrative up with one of the genre's most powerful bands to emerge in years, packing a punch with their songs that resonated with listeners. Nose-to-nose with the exploitive music industry establishment that Ann and Nancy could have laid down for, as many of their predecessors had done in the past to be largely used as objects of sexual desire, Heart instead stood proud and

'When it got personal,
we fought back with rock.'

worked to even the score for women in rock.

Packaging messages of change in pop hits was not a new phenomenon. Artists like Bob Dylan and Creedence Clearwater Revival had pioneered that a decade earlier in the 1960s, and dozens of politically charged pop anthems had followed, helping to bring an end to the Vietnam War and advance equal rights. Growing up amid the change as the children of hippie parents, Ann and Nancy had witnessed firsthand the power music could play in inspiring, shaping and, in some cases, defining broad societal change. While just about everyone else had been spoken for on record and radio, women as a social group had been largely ignored until the start of the 1970s, when the Wilson sisters were coming into their own as songwriters. In explaining what drove the creative social consciousness that showed up so poignantly and potently in Heart's albums of the late '70s, Nancy articulated that "as writers and as women, we were always aware of the imbalance of how the lion's share of earnings and credibility was largely awarded to the opposite sex. [When] we . . . chose to dwell on it . . . it really got personal as in 'Barracuda' or 'Even it Up.' When it got personal, we fought back with rock."

Consider *Rolling Stone*'s observation that "in the seventies . . . the Wilson sisters produced some of the only American prog-rock tunes— 'Magic Man,' 'Barracuda' and 'Crazy on You' — that have stood up to the British competition." Lead singer Ann explained to a journalist at the time that she felt the sisters' edge came from the fact that "we have a bond between us of not only love but a musical bond that is universal and, I think, pretty timeless. We were maybe *the* first pair of women to come out and say, 'We don't know the rules so we're not going to follow them.' I think a lot of people want to see what it is that we do that

nobody else does." Re-invent-
ing the marketplace for
women in rock as they went
along, the band would be put
through a trial by fire by the
very system that was supposed
to be working on its behalf. In
the way it promoted and mar-

> 'We don't know the rules
> so we're not going to
> follow them.'

keted the group, Heart's own label would act in glaring
contradiction to the message of the band's music. Heart's greatest power to combat that reality wasn't on stage, but rather in the
studio. Initially, the group intended to follow up *Dreamboat
Annie* not with *Little Queen*, their second studio release, but
rather with a protest album of sorts entitled *Magazine*.

The group had begun work on the new album during breaks
in the tour supporting their previous album. Still signed to
indie label Mushroom Records, while Heart was out on the road
and out of the loop, their label was promoting *Dreamboat Annie*
to radio and retail. The clash between the band and its label, as
Ann recalled it, came when "*Magazine* was three-quarters
recorded. We were touring when we first saw the Mushroom
Records' adverts for *Dreamboat Annie* in the States. They were
full-page tabloid pages of outtakes from the DBA cover shoot
with captions that suggestively said, 'It was only our first time.'
Today we recognize this level of demeaning lechery as *Girls
Gone Wild*. It was creepy . . . icky. Nancy and I were angry and
humiliated, and we hit back. 'Pull this stuff back,' we said. 'Shut
up and tour,' they said. We grew increasingly unhappy with the
way we were being portrayed, and while none of the men
around us seemed to mind, we *really* minded." So much so that
they halted further recording so the label couldn't acquire any
more masters. Heart began legal proceedings to sever their contract with Mushroom Records.

The impetus to leave Mushroom may have begun with

> ‘We do *not* want to be marketed this way; this hurts our music.’

lifelong friend Sue Ennis: “I think I may be guilty of setting off their rage at one point. They were in Europe doing a short tour, and while they were gone, Mushroom Records took out an ad in *Rolling Stone*. It was an outtake from the *Dreamboat Annie* cover that looked a little salacious, where Ann and Nancy seemed to be looking longingly at each other. The ad copy read, ‘It was only our first time,’ and the insinuation was that they were sister-lesbians. Even though it was supposed to be referring to the first time they made an album, there was no doubt what was being suggested. When they came back, I was all up in arms, and was feeling protective of them. I was saying, ‘This is not okay to be marketed this way.’ That’s the first time I showed them the ad without saying anything, they went, ‘Huh, yeah well that’s cool. The label took out a full-page ad.’ I said, ‘Yeah, but look,’ and pointed out the sexual angle, and they just flipped out. They were calling their label, saying, ‘We do *not* want to be marketed this way; this hurts our music.’ Because it wasn’t what they were about and it was embarrassing to their family. It hurt and was maddening on so many levels. So that was maybe the first time they realized they could be exploited to sell records in that way, and I think the trigger event for them leaving Mushroom was that ad, and then everything that followed with *Magazine*.”

As producer Mike Flicker recalled, “Conceptually the girls had already come up with *Magazine*, which was really the embodiment of probably the same thing we fight today: the struggle that women have as girls, growing up with one image that you open a magazine and see with models dictating what they should look and act like. And Ann and Nancy had fallen victim to some of that in their career thus far at the hands of the record label and promoters. So whenever the band was interviewed, no one ever wanted to talk to the guys in the band, just Ann and Nancy. And whenever they did interview the sisters, the interviewer only wanted to talk about superficial stuff. I also think it was a deeper, personal concept [speaking] to the fact that growing up they fell victim to

'. . . we always felt powerful and effective as well as tender and vulnerable.'

it themselves as fans. So I think the album concept was a reflection more of their personal lives than their professional lives, and a deeper, intellectual feeling, but incorporated elements of both. But to sort of that point in their career till about the middle to the end of *Little Queen*, I think there was more culling from their personal life before stardom than there was of their life after stardom. And I would say my personal belief is that's a beauty of the songwriting to that point. So when *Magazine*'s recording got interrupted, it almost became what I would term an abortion of that concept. What happened was we only recorded the first four or five basic tracks, hadn't even done any overdubs, because we were still constructing the album. Then the lawsuit happened between Heart and Mushroom, and the band left and signed to CBS Records. There had been certain promises made regarding the marketing of the group, which had to do with the conceptual subject of *Magazine*, that the girls would not be marketed as a piece of meat."

Nancy explained that Heart chose to make its mark, and its point, through its music, "All throughout the shifts and arcs of culture, Ann and I always tried to keep our heads above water as far as championing or being poster girls for the cause of equality of the sexes. We just put our heads down and worked hard to change things by showing up and making our mark instead of politicking. I think it's tough enough for anyone artistic, not just women. In the spirit of our music, we always felt powerful and effective as well as tender and vulnerable. That's the duality of Heart. Damn the torpedoes!"

Signing to a major label was appropriate to the band's popularity at the time, but their battle with Mushroom was a reflection of just how hard the Wilson sisters would have to work to change the system from within. First on their list of priorities was writing and recording a new album, which would build upon the concept of *Magazine*, but make even more of a mockery of the role female singers had traditionally been forced to play on album covers, as though they enjoyed and encouraged their own sexual exploitation. Titling the album *Little Queen* poignantly poked fun at that norm, but writing and recording in a whirlwind of touring and litigation made this a less-than-light-hearted experience for the Wilson sisters.

Mike Flicker recalled the enormous difficulties the band faced: "Aside from time constraints, there was a lawsuit going on at that point. The band was changing labels, and people were threatening to keep them from recording at all. Another dynamic that changed was when we recorded *Little Queen*, they'd be on tour, so we'd record, they'd go out on tour again, and have three days here and two days there. When we went in to record *Little Queen*, the lawyer had sat us down and said, 'There's a hearing in three weeks, and at that hearing, we don't know if you're going to be stopped from completing *Little Queen* until the lawsuit is settled, or not. It's going to be up to a panel of nine federal judges.' Mushroom was seeking a temporary restraining order to stop Heart from doing any more recording at all till the lawsuit was settled. So the lawyer said, 'But, if you actually get the album on the streets before then, the chances are way, way in your favor that the judge is not going to stop it.' So they gave us our choice, and the group decided they were going to finish the album [before the hearing]. So there hit a point where we'd maybe only recorded less than half the album, and were told we had to deliver the

album in three weeks. There were three or four things that had been recorded by that point that were supposedly going to be part of another album, *Magazine* (which ended up coming out later due to the lawsuit). We'd recorded four or five cuts of *Magazine*, and were continuing working on what we thought was that album, when the band suddenly changed record labels. So the songs we had recorded for *Magazine* became unavailable to the band legally. Thankfully, we hadn't quite recorded 'Barracuda' yet, but we had written that thinking it was part of *Magazine*. We'd rehearsed it, gotten it ready, but hadn't gotten in the studio yet. Luckily, because 'Barracuda' had not been recorded yet, we still had rights to it." For Ann, the biggest frustration artistically was the bottom line that "Mushroom went to court to stop us from finishing *Magazine*."

Given their time constraints for recording, Heart was at least ahead of the game with writing the album's material. The band had been working double-time on the road, writing songs in between shows. As Flicker, who doubled as the group's live sound engineer, recalled: "The band was touring a lot during these second and third albums, and I would usually be out on the road with them, doing live sound and then we'd rehearse new songs, and a lot of times sit down on a day off and they'd play songs they'd been working on. In a certain sense, I think my presence was support, but I was also trying to keep a grasp on the evolution of the band itself. A lot of times it would be me and Ann, or me and Ann and Nancy — it was mostly Ann and I — on days off, or before a show, just sitting around talking about the concepts of the album. Where were we going? Here's the songs, and here's some of their thoughts.

"On *Dreamboat Annie*, I had had more of the creative reigns, not out of anything other than experience. But as we went along, the girls were extremely quick learners. They watched me develop with them the concept of 'Dreamboat Annie' and the album. Then, the next concept became *Magazine*, and whereas

Dreamboat Annie was more of a collaborative concept, with *Magazine*, they talked to me one day and said, 'We have a concept for an album.' So that's how quick — from album number one where it was collaborative to album number two where they sat me down and said, 'We understand what you did, and so now, how do you like this idea?' *Magazine* was really the first concept that was totally born out of their brains. So it disappointed me very much that it got off track, because we're in the process, going along, and management had been telling us in the midst of moving from Mushroom to CBS, 'It shouldn't be a big deal,' and the worse scenario was we may lose those performances and would have to re-record the songs. That didn't seem like such a big deal compared to the plus side, but what happened was everything got frozen, and the group wasn't even allowed to re-record those same songs. So after getting over the shock of that, we started creating the next album, which became *Little Queen*, on the road. Looking back, it's a real sore spot for me, and I'm sure for them still; *Little Queen* came from the additional songs that were originally written for *Magazine*, such as 'Barracuda' and 'Dream of the Archer,' so *Little Queen* as an album then became a backwards concept."

The urgency of the three-week timeline drove the aggression and energy of the band's performances during the *Little Queen* recording sessions. From a producer's perspective, Flicker recalled the compressed schedule: "For three weeks I had the group recording in two studios at one time, where I was running from doing a vocal in one room to listening to a guitar solo in the other room. Then when some songs were finished, I would be mixing in one room, then running in and listening to overdubs in the other. A lot of the energy you hear in that album's tracks reflects the frenzy of that recording schedule. It was a nat-

> 'Looking back, it's a real sore spot for me.'

'. . . there was no time for reflection. It was a war.'

ural reflection of the pace we were working at, plus there was a certain intent by the group of saying, 'Hey Mike, we want this to be more of a group album, and we want it to be less of a polished album.' That album was a specific reaction, so you didn't have to talk about what was going on to motivate the energy in the performances, because it was in the air 24/7. The girls' performance on that album was different because everything was done with a sense of urgency, and there was no time for reflection. It was a war."

Guitarist Howard Leese noted the striking difference in the mood of the recording sessions from the previous album to *Little Queen*: "When we'd made *Dreamboat Annie*, we weren't trying to make a hit record; the band just wanted to make a record. They were just thrilled to be in the studio making a real album, with that wonderful naiveté of a band's first recorded work, and they were not famous at the time and coming out of nowhere. By the time we did *Little Queen*, the band was already getting to be successful, and there was all that legal mumbo-jumbo going on in the background, so there was some anger among band members about that whole business thing as a distraction. Another thing that was different about recording that album was, by that time, the band had moved back home to Seattle, which is where we recorded the album. The thing I remember most about that was the room we recorded in was about a sixth as big as the room at Mushroom Studios, so we're all in there together, working under all this pressure."

Reasoning that the greatest way to combat their old label was to produce an atomic bomb of a hit record, Ann and Nancy Wilson wrote "Barracuda" as an ode to the industry sharks they had fought against their entire way up the charts. As Ann explained to a journalist, "'Barracuda' was just a real angry song about Nancy and I realizing firsthand how sleazy the record business was when we first got into it. We weren't treated with any credibility at all. We were out there working really hard and being treated like cheesecake items and they made us all really angry. . . . It's a song that still contains all the angst

we felt when we wrote it . . . I think [it's] . . . another one that has kept all its molecules together really well with the passage of time . . . because it still has all its rage. . . . [It] just has stood the test of time. It's just as pissed off now as it was when it was written." Sue Ennis, for her part, explained, "It wasn't as though they had a broader plan to become leaders of the women's liberation movement. They had no agenda, and weren't trying to prove anything. But 'Barracuda' kind of took on a life of its own as a protest anthem against sexism. That song was about a specific record executive who said something vile to Ann after a show one night. Afterward, she seethed, 'That guy was such a barracuda!' So it was about the typical record guy who just wants to make money off you, and at that point, Ann and Nance were calling each other 'Porpoise' for whatever reason, and so that line in the song where Ann sings, 'You met the porpoise and me,' wasn't all that veiled. But the song was about that one incident, and I don't think they meant to make a giant statement with it."

Further describing how that rage in the air translated to recording the song, Leese recalled that "the clearest memory I have of that vibe and atmosphere was recording 'Barracuda.' We worked on it and worked on it and worked on it, and it was a very complicated song rhythmically. There's a lot of funny math in that song — funny bars, beats of seven, beats of five, beats of nine. There were a number of different sections to the song, and to keep it clear to ourselves we named each section after a fish. So it was two salmons and a tuna, then back to the salmon, then to the barracuda section. Originally, 'barracuda' was just one of the many fish sections, but it just happened to stick. Then the girls had a promo guy we'd met that they really, really didn't like, so they wrote the lyrics about him, and instead of calling him a shark or a wolf or the usual derogatory animal name, they called him a barracuda, because all of the parts of the songs had different fish names. So we worked on that song for a long time because it is so complicated, and I just remember slugging it out in that little studio, going over all the different fish parts, and coming up with a track that made sense.

"To date, I think it's one of the weirdest songs to end up in the top ten, and one of only three with that many weird tempos. There's Dave Brubeck's 'Take 5,' Pink Floyd's 'Money,' and us. So I'm real proud of that, having a hit song with that many beats in it. To this day, it's still the song everybody brings up. The other cool thing was we tracked the song 100 percent live in the studio, even the vocal, because Ann was singing live with us while we were recording the track so we'd know where we were. Then we'd go back and maybe fix a couple things on the vocal. But pretty much everything on that album is live, except at the very end, there are some Mellotron strings I added, and some of the crazy sound effects Roger put on there. Everything else was pretty live. Ann didn't like any effect on her voice when she was singing, delay only. She would use one bounce of delay at about 350 milliseconds, basically Led Zeppelin — 'Hey, hey. . . . Hey, hey.' She didn't like reverb on her voice, she didn't like that cathedral sound, she just wanted to go 'Hey, hey,' with one bounce about half as loud as the original one. One slap. The guitar rig I used on all our early albums was a 1966 Telecaster. That was my main guitar back then, and my amp was a 1956 Fender 410 Bassman, and for micing, we usually just put a 57 in front of it. That's as basic as it gets, and that's what I used for the first five records, all those hits, including 'Barracuda.'"

Expanding on the technical side of the song's recording process, Flicker explained that "'Barracuda' wasn't recorded at Mushroom Studios, which was different for me. It was a different console and different studio. After they'd gone on tour for a while and after I'd recorded some of the stuff for *Magazine*, they wanted to move back home to Seattle. And I knew this, so I had an opportunity at the time to make a deal with a studio down in Seattle which allowed me to go in and make some adjustments to their room, which mainly involved making it live. It had been one of those '70s Westlake rooms that basically was like walking inside of a marshmallow. The studio at the time was called 'K Smith Studios,' and so they allowed me to go in and start from scratch. So I gutted the room, and did as much as we could in the space to make it live. We ended up having to record 'Barracuda' in their other studio because the one I was working on wasn't ready yet.

"I ended up using the same mic set-up for 'Barracuda' that I had on *Dreamboat Annie*, but the kit was different because by then we were using a hybrid. Michael Derosier was still letting me use some of my drums, and he was using some of his drums. So what we did was I built almost like a room for his bass drum, because he wanted to use the double-headed, and to get a little bit more concussion, he allowed me to cut a little hole in his bass drum. And so I did a thing where I was able to isolate the bass drum in what looked like a little tunnel in front of it. For that set-up, I used a RA20 mic right directly on the bass drum, then I had a 57 mic on his beater with a gate to get the attack, and finally had a 414A as a distant mic. For the guitars on that song, there was a particular flanger which was an experimental thing that a friend of Roger's had built. It never actually saw the light of day outside of 'Barracuda.' It was in this aluminum box with knobs and whatever, and just had an extreme flanger that really helped that crunchy guitar sound. We've never gotten that guitar mic since. What was kind of experimental about it was it sat between the pre-amp and the power amp, so Roger actually had a jack built into his Marshall where you could take the pre-amp out and do direct sounds. So it came out of that, into this flanger, out of the flanger and back into the power amp. Then Howard had his own flanger that he used for his rig, and they flanged up a storm together. There were three guitar tracks on that song including Nancy, who played an Ovation, which was miced and direct. As with *Dreamboat*, my electric guitar mic of choice was an M69. My theory with mixing guitars, with that song and all the other Heart songs, was if you had one guitar part that does the trick, you can turn it up louder, and it will do more. So less is more kind of theory, which I always felt was The Beatles' success. George Martin would have 12 guitars doing one part, so that you never really heard any of them over another. So that's how I mixed the guitars on 'Barracuda.' Whenever we'd do rhythm, power, acoustic guitar — and I think this is something I developed that became a trademark — most of the time it was three guitars at once, and I would record Nancy, Howard and Roger playing acoustic guitar, mic it all live, and put it on one stereo track. That kind of positioned them the way I wanted to hear it so they'd get the balance. That was stationary throughout the early stuff on *Dreamboat Annie*, *Little Queen* and *Magazine*."

While the producer may have had some norms developed for recording Heart's guitar sound, Mike Flicker found that producing the album as a whole held more challenges than with the band's debut. "Where I had taken time in *Dreamboat Annie*, where I would do performances, then say, 'Let's move onto another song, and come back to it in three weeks, and I'll reflect back and see if this is really what we want, or can we do better?' Also, I used more production elements on *Dreamboat Annie* that was absent on *Little Queen* because it was a conscious effort on the band's part to be a straight-up rock record. Their manager used to have a saying, 'There are two kinds of albums: come buy and come see. You can make the kind of album where people want to come and buy the album, or one where people want to come and see you live.' And their intent was to make a *come-see* album. I saw it more as they wanted a less-produced, as far as polished, more raw and more of a group sound, which was not what I was going after on the first album because there wasn't yet a group. So I produced with a less-is-more theory, and more toward a live vibe. I always felt like the role of a producer, generally, and specifically with them, was more like the director of a movie, who's trying to direct a performance. Having that opportunity to spend a year and a half ahead of this through the whole evolution of recording the first album, and they respond intellectually to things, and by then, they got it. And the thing that struck a chord with them was — before we even sang — I talked to them conceptually about the fact that, to me, every song is like a script and a mini-movie. And the vocalist is the lead performer. I believe a singer has to put themselves into character when it's time to go in and record the vocal, and so that's why we've always spent time talking about songs, and making sure, at the beginning, that we all understood. And as things progressed, they would take the lead in that, so that when trying to get the performance, I knew conceptually where the song was coming from. But because of time [constraints recording *Little Queen*], it was a different approach, because with our deadline it was also literally like working in a war zone. And there was a change in attitude toward the music, on the part of the band as a whole. It was all about the music, and not about the band and anything else when we did *Dreamboat Annie*, which given the circumstances and everything, makes a lot of sense. Then they went on the road and became a band; before *Dreamboat Annie* there really wasn't a band, and there was no 'Let's do this part because it's better for this person, or the sound, or we're trying to create a sound for the band, or how will this play live?' There wasn't any

consideration of that; it was strictly making a record. It was about the music. Then, rightfully, they became a band, so *Little Queen* was more about making a band record."

Putting an album together — recording, tracking and mixing — in three weeks was a near impossible task but one that Heart and its producer were determined to achieve, even if by the skin of their teeth. Describing the urgency, Ann recalled that "it was a Friday night; the deadline for stopping work was Monday morning. We stayed at the studio, eating, sleeping under the desk until it was done in the wee hours of Monday morning, at which time Mike Flicker got on a plane with the tapes ready for release. It was a rush job, and you can hear it, but it still contains some great moments." Flicker jumped on the chartered jet "that flew directly from Seattle to Santa Maria, California, where the album was being pressed. So I went from Seattle to Los Angeles, had it mastered, and then out to the plant in Santa Maria in less than 24 hours to meet our deadline, and we just made it."

Heart's new label, CBS Records, released *Little Queen* in May 1977 to eager fans who instantly drove the album into the Top 10 of Billboard's Pop Album Chart, and turned "Barracuda" into a Top 10 AM radio smash single. *Rolling Stone* was as caught up in the album's infectious energy as the band's fan base, noting in their review that "lead singer Ann Wilson, with her urgent, often explosive vocals, is the closest rock has to a female counterpart of Zeppelin's Robert Plant." The magazine went on to positively comment that "*Little Queen* ups the heavy quotient on hits like 'Barracuda' with satisfying results. . . . Heart's follow-up to their phenomenally successful debut LP continues their . . . marriage of bursting-at-the-seams hard rock and reflective, soft acoustic music." The magazine concluded by correctly predicting "there's little doubt that *Little Queen* will do well financially."

Whether Mushroom Records took note of the magazine's comment specifically, or the band's ever-rising popularity, the label decided to recoup its initial investment in Heart's aborted *Magazine* LP by releasing an unauthorized and unfinished version, which featured five demos and some live-board sound recordings. This infuriated Heart even further, causing the group to respond with an additional lawsuit seeking to have the bootleg LP pulled from store shelves. In the frenzy that followed, an eventual compromise was worked out between Heart and their former label, by the courts. Ann explained, "Mushroom had rushed out their own version of *Magazine* filled out with studio musicians and singers. We were livid and went to court to have it withdrawn. The judge saw things our way, and the Mushroom version of *Magazine* was pulled off the shelves and replaced with ours. All this legal wrangling and emotional hand-wringing took its toll on the music and on us. We were always touring. We were just anxious to get on with it." In a déjà-vu of the compressed *Little Queen* recording sessions, the band was given seven days to record *Magazine*'s additional tracks and to complete the original *Magazine* demos. Flicker explained, "What happened was, for the album *Magazine*, we had recorded four or five studio tracks, before *Little Queen*, when the lawsuit happened, which put those tracks — 'Heartless,' 'Devil Delight,' 'Just the Wine' and 'Magazine' — on hold. I liked those songs, and the basic tracks were keepers, and intended to be records. Everybody was a little wide-eyed too, and had thought that those first songs we'd already recorded for Mushroom Records would become available to us eventually, which they didn't. What happened was, after we recorded the basic tracks for four or five songs, and during the lawsuit, we had also done some live broadcasts from clubs. So we had tapes of these live broadcasts, and they were never meant to be recordings. They were supposed to be for radio, but it was the label's idea to record them. And then the radio station would allow us to go back into the studio and do a remix before broadcast. But because they were never intended to be used on a studio album, no care was taken in that regard, although there was a certain spirit to the performances. So what eventually happened was that in the process of all this litigation, Mushroom Records actually put out a version of *Magazine*, with the same songs that are on the proper *Magazine* LP as you hear it today, but without us. So basically the person who was my second engineer, Rolf Henneman, still worked for Mushroom, and they send him into the studio with the rough vocals, the scratch vocals that were sung during the tracking. Ann always sang, everything was always done live, so there were vocals, but they were what we called 'scratch vocals,' and so they had taken all that and turned it into an album and released it, which naturally pissed everyone off. So it took us about two days to find out it happened; the lawyers went to court, got an injunction and got it stopped, but meanwhile out there were about 100,000 copies of this thing. What they had done was an end-run, and released it from their European distributor, Arista Records, and imported about 40,000 or 50,000 into the United States. So who knows how many got stocked. They were ordered by the court to be destroyed and burned. So what happened was the lawsuit got settled, and part of the settlement was the group was given one week to go in to finish the rough tracks, and we were limited in what we were allowed to do — lead vocals and lead guitars. We weren't allowed to touch the live radio tracks, but we could remix them. So we were allowed to do as much as we could to them, all in one week. So it was a marathon, sleeping at the studio, but we got it done."

The band was understandably frustrated. "By then, we were trying to be real artistic, and we had just done *Little Queen*, which we thought was artistically valid, and had some interesting stuff on there," recalled Leese. "So to all of a sudden have to jump back in and work on stuff we'd done a couple years ago was kind of jarring, but better than the version the record company had. They had brought in some local studio guys to finish it, and only had half the record we'd done for them before the band went into litigation. So they tried to finish it, and then slapped some live stuff from one of our first club appearances on there. And so we didn't feel that was very representative of us, but knew we couldn't stop it from coming out at some point, and figured it would be better for us to go in and try to clean it up and finish it ourselves, rather than have ghost guys on there. That really offended us. So we had to jump in and finish five tracks, and it was conflicting for Mike Flicker and me because we were two of the three guys who had originally started the Mushroom label. At some point, when I joined the band, I had to stop being management, and start being labor. I was no longer a part of the label when I joined the band, so it was a strange time for me. Anyway, it was nice to get the tracks back so we could finish them, and I did the piano solo at the end of 'Magazine,' and one of the other things that was cool was on 'Devil Delight,' I got to bring in my new toy, which was an Arp Avatar guitar synthesizer that had just been invented, and I had just gotten one from the company. So I added a little bit of guitar synthesizer on that song, and the record came out a month later, and I was the first guy to have a guitar synth come out and be on a record. We only had about a week to go in and work on the record, between touring. We had a deadline from Mushroom for how long we could have the tapes before they were going to put it out, so it was not very artistic." The album was a hit in spite of its rushed finish and incomplete concept, far from the original idea Ann described as "this incredible concept package with a page for each song, designed like a magazine except deeper."

> 'It was a sweet home-coming, and it was then, too, that things really started happening.'

Re-released in early spring 1978, *Magazine* went platinum, but the band had already moved on. With the album's release, Heart had no further obligations to Mushroom; the band "was free [from] the legal battle of our career that threw off the rhythm of the quality and release of our follow-up to *Dreamboat Annie*," summed up Ann. "It was a sweet homecoming, and it was then, too, that things really started happening. . . . We started writing and recording . . . a new album, a new label. Another chance in smooth waters." In spite of the headway the sisters had made in their battle with their label, Ann's optimism looking forward and the platinum-selling success of their first three LPs, Nancy remained skeptical: "the late '70s were only a warm-up as far as the image-making experts were concerned. We had just stepped out from the amazing cultural revolution of the late '60s where the focus was talent and imagination. By the '80s and MTV, it was mostly all over. But fashion and music always does need to mutate and shift focus. Big shake-ups seem to come along at the beginning of each decade."

Describing the band's mood from a friend's perspective, Sue Ennis recalled, "I was in California at Berkeley, and they were making [*Little Queen*] in Seattle, and they would call me and say, 'This is going well. We're at this great studio that is so cool.' It was a good, exciting time, and I remember coming home for a break from school when they invited me to the studio and you know what surprised me? Ann and Nance were all dressed up! Like, well, like 'ladies.' They'd just received a bit of money as a signing bonus from Portrait Records and had bought some designer dresses! Ann had a fondness for Diane von Furstenberg, and she looked gorgeous but I couldn't understand the heels and the dark stockings. Looking back, I think they were experimenting with being able to afford haute couture for the first time. And I imagine they were getting great reviews from the guys in the band. For a good chunk of time as they recorded *Little Queen*, Ann and Nance really got dolled up to go to the studio every day. One night we were at Mike's house, and they played early mixes of 'Say Hello,' 'Little Queen' and 'Barracuda' for me. They were very proud of the songs, and once again, the Wilson sisters blew me away!"

With the public now aware of the band's legal entanglements, critics were impressed with what the band had pulled off with the re-worked *Magazine*. *Rolling Stone* noted that while "Mushroom Studios' . . . stench of deception reeks . . . [even now that] they released the completed Heart tracks with enough shameless, inferior but authorized padding to look like an album-length effort. . . . Nonetheless, hard-core Heart fans shouldn't be deterred." The magazine concluded that it was clear the world was watching and listening as "Heart . . . realize[s] the potential of its obvious talents." For its next LP, Heart would try to produce an album entirely free of the pressures that had faced its second and third.

CHAPTER 6

Dog and Butterfly

1978

By 1978, Heart had amassed enough commercial capital to fully spread its creative wings, and produce its most mature and personal album to date, *Dog and Butterfly*. Encapsulating the band's achievement with this LP, *Rolling Stone* stated, "In the man's world of hard rock, [Heart's] orientation is feminine. . . . Their success could be interpreted as blows against the empire. But none of this matters anymore. . . . *Dog and Butterfly* is Heart as a whole: they haven't plastered over the contradictions in their ideas of women's rock, they've lived up to and beyond them."

In seeking to conceptually heighten and enlighten their writing for the fourth LP even further, the sisters enlisted childhood friend Sue Ennis as their lyrical partner, a natural choice, as Nancy explained. "She and Ann met in high school when they discovered a mutual love of The Beatles. We started playing guitars like fiends right away, but she was too shy about performing to join up with any of our early fledgling bands. We started collaborating with our lifelong friend Sue Ennis during the *Dog and Butterfly* era. It was behind the scenes where she flourished as a co-writer and was always a source of great friendship and support through the extreme roller coaster rides of our lives. Sue Ennis is an amazing friend and writer." From producer Mike Flicker's point of view, enlisting an outside writer didn't change the fundamentals of Heart's winning songwriting formula. In terms of how Ennis's presence affected the Wilson sisters as writers, Flicker recalled, "I never felt it was a hugely creative injection, other than how it allowed the girls to feel about their creativity."

For her part, Ennis recalled the beginning of what would become an involved partnership in Heart's songwriting: "I was in Berkeley, and they came to San Francisco to play a concert, and they had some time before the show, and came over in their limo to my little place in Berkeley. And they'd been on the road so I hadn't seen them for like seven months. They walked up to my door looking like rock stars — with these perms, and fantastic leather jackets, and great boots. So when I opened the door, we all laughed, like, 'Oh my God, look at you!' We spent that afternoon in my little pad there in Berkeley with guitars, and we had a really fantastic time, sitting around drinking tea, playing old songs and getting caught up. And I remember they were really tired. They told me, 'Epic wants a record in three months; we haven't written a thing. We're kinda burnt from the road.' And also, I think, a little aspect of their exhaustion came from their being the only women in the tour, traveling constantly for like seven months, with 30 guys. They just had each other. I think they also found it fun that afternoon to just be effortless in the company that we had. They pulled out the beginnings of a song they were just sketching out at that point, and it was called 'Dog and Butterfly.'"

As Ann explained to a journalist, the inspiration for the album's title track came very simply: "Looking out my window [I] saw my old sheepdog and she was trying to catch a butterfly and you know dogs can't catch them that easily, especially big old dogs like that. But it struck me as being like I was in my quest for writing the perfect song or having success in the rock business, or what anyone's thing is that they're trying to achieve and it keeps evading them. So once again, I took a simple thing and put it on a higher level."

"I remember Ann showing me the lyrics," recalled Ennis on the writing process for "Dog and Butterfly." "They played me what they had, and I thought it was great. Then they asked, 'God, what would we do for a bridge?' and I made a couple of suggestions. It was just natural to put in my two cents based on our long musical history. So then at the end of the afternoon, Ann said, 'Do you mind if we put your name on this?' And I said, 'Oh, that would be cool,' but didn't understand it meant I was an official co-writer on the song yet. Anyway, I remember when they left, we were all exhilarated from our reunion, and the music and new song, and they said, 'We gotta come back and write some more songs together.'"

Flicker explained that while "Sue wasn't in the picture at the beginning, she was basically a childhood friend of both Ann and Nancy, and they used to play guitar and sing together, the three of them, and hung out together as teenagers. So there really was a foundation of trust. Then they went off to do their thing, she moved to the Bay area and went to Berkeley. Then as the band became more successful, the girls reunited, and that's exactly what they found in her — in a certain respect I felt they, at first, were almost looking for her approval, and that weaned itself into a collaboration. So it was a trust and respect between them." Nancy described their collaborative process: "We'd fly to Berkeley where [Sue] was a grad student and hole up with acoustic guitars and notebooks in a good hotel for the weekend.

'Mistral Wind' was written in this way, and even though I had most of the music in place, the lyrics took all weekend. The three of us wrote as an equal lyric team."

A routine for the writing sessions developed, as Ennis described: "They'd head off for a bit back to Seattle, but would come back to San Francisco over weekends when I was free. A limo would come get me, and take me across the Bay Bridge to a fantastic hotel in downtown San Francisco. It was always the Stanford Court or the Mark Hopkins or The Fairmont. We'd get in there on Friday nights, and not come out till Sunday evening when we had a new song. We ordered room service all weekend long but didn't want any outside people, like waiters, hanging around. One thing we always ordered was the 'tableside Caesar salad.' But we didn't want them doing the big presentation of making the salad in front of us in the room. So we told them to please just make it up in the kitchen. We also asked them to just knock on the door, leave the cart in the hallway, but they wouldn't do that. We had a joke that we should also tell them to walk away, without turning around when they heard the door open. That's how much we wanted to be left alone. When Ann and Nance and I were writing, Ann was always our scribe, but I think for that album, we hammered out most of the lyrics together. We'd be sitting around tossing out lines, and the ones that were obviously pretty good, she'd write down, then we'd say, 'Oh, we need a rhyme for this.' And we'd come up with the worst rhymes in the world and most trite lines, laughing all the way to something good. Afterward, Ann and Nancy took the new song back to Seattle, and during the week, they called me from the studio, excited, saying, 'Listen to how it's coming along!' So Ann and Nance would make little cassette tapes of our songs as we wrote them, and then play them for Flicker and the rest of the band. Just stripped down songs: chords, melodies and lyrics. The band guys would stand around and listen, and when it was over, no one would say anything! Afterward, Ann and Nance called me

Ann Wilson and Sue Ennis

and I'd say, 'So, what did the guys think of the song?' They told me, 'Well, no one said anything.' And the three of us would joke, like, how can you not respond to somebody who's laying their soul on the line, completely vulnerable? Couldn't they at least say, 'Oh, cool,' or 'Okay, I can work with that?' But I think they didn't want to acknowledge that the girls had written the song. So that was something that was always hard for us, on every album after that, being the female writing team, bringing a tune to some dudes who figured they were strictly rock guys. And maybe it was their job in a way to dismiss the girly lyrics and stuff; it gave them a sense of power. I should say that Howie was always the most open and collaborative. It can't have been all that easy for the guys to be in a women-fronted band where the Wilsons got most of the attention. So on that album, my input was more in the writing process than the recording process."

In identifying some of her favorite collaborations the trio created for the *Dog and Butterfly* LP, Nancy seized on "'Mistral Wind' . . . one of the most iconic Heart greats. I think the music

'. . . it was a bit of a metaphor for the writing process too: waiting for inspiration.'

balances with and describes the words in a rare way." Also a favorite of her sister, Ann explained to one journalist that "'Mistral Wind' and 'Dog and Butterfly' [are my favorites]. . . . I guess it really has come down to the boys and the girls in Heart. . . . We didn't purposely set out that way, but that's the way it's worked out, 'cause the girls write the songs, and we all live together, and we're old friends. We don't try to beat 'em down or anything. We have boys who are very, very good musicians, but it doesn't necessarily mean we're the creators." For co-writer Ennis, "'Mistral Wind' [was] one of the great experiences of our writing partnership, I think, because it felt like a mysterious song, almost like a mystery was leading us. It didn't start so much with 'We've got to write a song'; it was an exploration process, and the more we followed it, the more it seemed to reveal. But it really began from sitting around going, 'What do we write about?' At the time I was telling them about the French wind I had read about which blows through the south of France, and the myth is that it makes people crazy. When that mistral wind comes, people go nuts. And we started to build that idea, and as we were sitting there, waiting for some sort of inspiration to come, we got the idea of being on a ship. A failing ship where we were stranded, without wind. Then once the inspiration comes and the wind blows up, you're on your way. So it was a bit of a metaphor for the writing process too: waiting for inspiration. When they finished recording 'Mistral Wind' in the studio, I was completely thrilled, and live I thought it was even more powerful."

How the album's title track, "Dog and Butterfly," came to be not only a Heart classic but the concept for the album as a whole, Nancy once explained: "I'll never forget it as long as I live. In Ann's backyard, the big air-hole house . . . [she] lived in at the time [on Lake Washington] . . . It was one of those idyllic Seattle summers. Ann had written a whole poem about looking out of her window and seeing her sheepdog Moffa chasing a butterfly as sheepdogs do because they're always looking up at the sky trying to do the impossible. So we put it to music and we were steeped in a lot of Joni Mitchell and also Loggins and Messina's stuff. The *Full Sail* album. And so we just took our guitars out in the backyard and sat at [Ann's] picnic table and to the sound of the lake sort of lapping against the shore, we wrote that song. And finished it in a day. With [Ann's] words and our music. . . . It fit our band because our fans are usually split into two armies. The ones who liked the ballads and the ones who liked the rockers. We'd get letters that said, 'God, I wish you wouldn't play those god-awful sappy ballads, keep the rock comin'.' And the other letters were exactly the opposite." Continuing on how the song turned conceptually into a broader album, Ann explained in an interview that "when I write poetry, I write like a high school girl so it was in stanzas with a little bridge part, naturally. It felt right because the whole poem was about opposition and one trying to attain the other, which is impossible. We thought, hey, one side could be the 'dog' side of the album and one could be the 'butterfly' side. And the whole thing grew from there."

And the band had earned the artistic freedom to do as they pleased with the album conceptually, as Leese explained. "By then, this was our fourth record, and we were very successful already, playing in stadiums and doing very, very well. So by the time we went in to record *Dog and Butterfly*, we could pretty much do what we wanted to do, whatever we felt like doing, in being more artistic, which is what the band had always wanted to do in the first place. So I think we would look at Zeppelin and go, 'Well, they don't even release singles.' We wanted to make a great album and put out the whole album and let people dig the

> '*Dog and Butterfly* was the first album that they had a chance to really spread their creative wings.'

record. People are going to listen to it, if there's a single, great, if not, we never thought 'Barracuda' was a single either. That was never intended ahead of time to be a single."

With the writing largely completed, Heart moved into the recording studio bringing an atmosphere that was positive and confident. Flicker recollected, "Ann and Nancy did as much pre-arranging as they could, and they used to get together and jam the songs out. Recording by that point was a lighthearted thing in terms of the band's attitude; they had a sense of humor about it, and that made sense as it was their fourth studio record in three years and the lawsuit had been settled. Because they'd had some success, [recording] was a less-pressured affair. In a certain respect, after working on the early stuff — which to me is *Dreamboat Annie* through the first half of *Magazine* — things were at a certain creative level, in a good way, but the next creative phase was different. After the lawsuit, and the release of *Little Queen* and then *Magazine*, that to me was a whole phase of that aggressive/anger/intense making records out of a wartime environment. Then *Dog and Butterfly* became a reaction to that, where it was like, 'Okay, now we can take some time.' We spent about a year making that record, so *Dog and Butterfly* was the first album that they had a chance to really spread their creative wings."

The album's first batch of recording sessions were held at Ann Wilson's home, but as Leese explained, practical sonic considerations eventually interfered. "We started working on the record at Ann's house. Ann and Nancy were back home, where they'd grown up, and everybody had a house by then, so it was a really great time for the band. So we worked for a few months there, and brought in some equipment and tried to record it there, and it just didn't sound right. We recorded 'Mistral Wind' there, and ended up recording that song three different times because we couldn't get it to sound the way we wanted it to sound. So we ended up moving to a little studio in Seattle called Sea West, a little bitty hole in the wall studio." Once the band was settled into a proper recording studio, it went about mapping out the harder, electric (dog) and softer, acoustic (butterfly) sides of the album. "When we got to the point where we were ready to record *Dog and Butterfly*," Mike Flicker recalled, "I think it conceptually was a little bit of a reflection of the fact that there are two sides, that it's all about yin and yang, and it was an attempt to even go further in both directions. I think there's the dog and butterfly in everybody was our theory, so the record was supposed to reflect both the acoustic side of them, and the live side as a band." Nancy Wilson explained how the acoustic and electric arrangements were split up within the band: "the decision on who plays what part on record or on stage is purely all about who can bring the most personality to the part. I bring personality to acoustic parts naturally, as well as most of the electric rhythm. . . . We always defer to the song itself to tell us who plays what with the best feel."

Heart not only deferred to the song, but listened to their fans' reactions to the new music, as Flicker noted. "I was still occasionally going on the road, listening to songs, doing things with them. And they would break in new songs live sometimes without even telling people, they'd just play them in their shows, songs they had just written. Sometimes they would re-tool those songs based off the reaction of the crowd. 'Mistral Wind' was a song I heard live first, and usually I'm thinking in terms of both the band's playing and the audience reaction, because you can tell what the audience is vibing on from the group. To me, it's always been more about the song, so I would make mental notes when they were playing live." As with their first three albums, all of the band's basic instrumental tracks were recorded live off the floor. Guitarist Leese recalled the band's unusual set-up, "It got so hot in the studio because we were recording during the summer time, when we were usually on tour, so because it was so beautiful weather-wise and we wanted to be outside, we ran long chords and long headphones for everybody, and sat in the back parking lot, in a little rough semi-circle playing, leaving only our drummer Mike in the studio. And at the time, we'd all bought '56 Ford T-birds, so we had five T-birds parked in the alley, and we'd sit in a circle with our headphones on and recorded *Dog and Butterfly* pretty much like that, sitting outside with the drummer in the studio."

Given the layers of tracks that accompanied Heart's lush string sections and multiple guitar overdubs, producer Mike Flicker had developed an outside-the-box recording system, which he had begun at Mushroom and transferred back to Seattle by the time principal recording on *Dog and Butterfly* commenced. "At Mushroom Studios, we had something that was different for the times — relative to the whole batch of records I made with Heart. . . . We recorded *Dreamboat Annie* on 16 tracks, and at that time, most people were converting to 24 track, and the reason I didn't was because I didn't really care for the sound. We were also converting at that time — believe it or not — to 30 IPS [inches per second]. That had just been introduced. Prior to that, all the tape recorders were running at 15 inches per second, and the difference in frequency response, and also noise, and at that same time, a lot of people were using Dolby noise reduction, and the early versions of Dolby noise reduction . . . I personally didn't like the way it colored the sound, because it had the tendency of doing that. Basically, what Dolby used to do is break it into different sound bands — compress the sound, lift it above the noise floor, and expand the sound on the way out. So it would encode the recording, and the encoded recording would go on tape, then it would decode the recording coming out, so it had the tendency of coloring the sound.

"For me, the big breakthrough was when we went to 30 inches per second, and reduced the noise, because with analog tape, the tape noise is basically the magnetic particles. And the faster those particles are going by, the less apparent noise you hear, because the noise ends up going above our hearing. So I initially liked the sound of 15 inches per second, but didn't like the frequency response and the noise. But with 30 inches per second, what happens is a change not only in the high end, but you also end up with a problem of a change in the low end, which has to do with the width of the tape and the heads. 16 track was on a two-inch tape width; 24 track was also on a two-inch tape width, hence each track had to be smaller. And because it's smaller and goes by faster, you get less low-end frequency response, and you're also losing more high-end frequency response. *Dreamboat Annie*'s sound maintained good frequency response by spreading 16 tracks over two-inch, but you had a 50 percent loss at 24 tracks. So I chose to go 30 inches per second and to go on 16 tracks, and I really liked the sound. Then after *Dreamboat Annie*, when the group wanted to spread their wings a bit, they said, 'God, everybody else is using 24 track, and you're using 16 track; everybody else gets to keep two vocals, we only get one vocal.' The first record was, 'Well, whatever you say we trust you.' Then the compromise was made on the start of the recording of *Little Queen* where we went to 24 track, and ultimately I wasn't happy because on certain songs where I really wanted more lower end, like a slower song or the songs like 'Little Queen,' which was a song that to me never got where I wanted it because it didn't have the funky-bottom I would have liked to have, like I had gotten on 'Magic Man.' And it really was that same kind of a slower groove, versus a 'Barracuda,' which was a faster thing, and having too much low-end would get in your way. You want a nice, tight low-end on something like that. So in the meantime, when we were touring and such, I had had my first opportunities touring in Europe — [where they] were more advanced in doing music on television — [we did] a lot of great rock television shows . . . and in fact, Heart did their first music videos in Europe. Music videos were promotable things, and so what happened was, I saw for the first time video tape being used, where they were locking up video tape basically by locking up our audio machine to their video machine. Because we would record those shows live, and the multi-track was locked up to their multi-track video. When I came back to the States, I called some people and said, 'Why can't we lock up two audio with the same device,' using this thing called SYMPTI, which was a time code."

By the time of the band's fourth studio LP, Flicker had developed a set-up that would overcome these technical limitations not just for Heart but also for the wider recording industry. "I found and bought a system, and created a method that we started on *Dog and Butterfly* of recording the basic tracks on 16 track, allowing us to have that bottom end on the bass and the drums and everything, and then I locked up a 24 track to the 16 track. And to take it one step further, the other problem I had noticed over the years with analog tape was that it's a physical medium, and tape sheds. And whenever I'd go back to my multi-track, whenever it was time to mix — I don't care if it was 16 track, or 24 track — I could hear: this doesn't sound the way it did when I recorded it, now that we've done a million overdubs, and spent hours and hours running the tape through the tape head. There's a degradation of sound while you're recording on the master, because you're playing that master tape. So with my monitor mix, every time I'd set up the monitoring mix, I'd find I kept having to add more high-end and more high-end to the monitoring mix to make it sound the way I remember it sounding when I first recorded it. I just naturally always strived to make the sound quality better, to make the aesthetic quality the best it can always be. So when we started working on *Dog and*

Butterfly, what I did was I recorded the basic tracks on 16 track, after editing and putting it together, and deciding we had our take, I then striped it with time code, and made a clone of it, and made a monitoring track. Instead of using up all 24 tracks, I'd take the maybe 10 or 12 tracks I'd used for the basic track, and make myself a monitoring mix of maybe 6 tracks, on the 24 track, leaving 17 available for overdubs, and one for SYMPTI. Those open tracks tended to be taken up by guitars and vocals, things that were less low- and high-end significant. And then I'd put the 16 track on the shelf, and didn't take it out till it was time to mix. Then when it was time to mix, I would lock the two machines together, and used the 16 tracks off one machine, and the 12 tracks off the other machine, and as far as I was concerned, had the best of both worlds. It allowed me to have the sound I wanted, and then *Mix Magazine* did an article on it, and then a bunch of people started doing it, and went crazy and started doing it the opposite way. So the guys doing the Bee Gees went bananas, with one 24-track machine with nothing but vocals, and all of a sudden, people were able to do 70, 80 tracks. Nobody had done that up to that point, and right after that *Mix* article, everyone was doing it. So Heart went to the multiple, multi-track recording before anyone else had."

Another highlight of the album, for Flicker as a producer, was how synergized the band had become musically. "At this point, everyone in the band was pretty collaborative too — a guitar lead would be more Nancy, in terms of the arrangement." Still, while the band chipped in, guitarist Howard Leese recalled that a norm had developed with the Wilson sisters concerning songwriting: "The girls tend to keep the writing credits for themselves if they can. You may come up with a big part, but they'll go, 'That's just the arrangement, that song's already written.' They were quick learners, especially in the songwriting and publishing arena." In some instances, the final version of a song had less to do with its composition and more with its performance; Flicker offered the following as an example. "A song called 'Cook with Fire,' that they came up with, which was an example of something that I first heard them do live, and we went in the studio, and it just wasn't happening. It just didn't have the energy. So I said, 'This is crazy, let's go do the basic track live,' and that's what we did, because it required the energy of the band live working the crowd. When we recorded that, I brought in a lot of the same studio mics, but leaned — especially on the drums — more toward dynamics. I brought in different overheads. A lot of the band's live sound grew out of the way we recorded in the studio, so it wasn't that far away."

'Heart went to the multiple, multi-track recording before anyone else had.'

In spite of the relaxed atmosphere of recording bed tracks, when attention turned to tracking what many would come to feel were Ann's strongest vocal performances to date, she undertook a disciplined preparatory process, as her sister described: "Warming up for singing is huge. Ann swears by mega doses of buffered vitamin C, lots of water and warm tea plus mentholyptus cough drops." Once Ann was warmed up and ready to record, Nancy explained her set-up in the studio: "The music stand should have a light for lyrics and the room should not be bright. A candle or two is always good luck. Her voice is a true gift from above." Both sisters also know which microphones best record their voices. "In the studio, for vocal sounds, we love the old tube Neumann mics. My voice records well with a tube Sound Delux." The sisters do differ in one aspect of making an album: mixing. As Nancy explained, "mixing for me is really exciting, whereas for Ann I'm sure it's more like watching grass grow. I'm a studio dog! I enjoy the process." And Sue Ennis added, "I think they enjoyed the recording process a lot, especially when something would click and take the song to the next level. I don't think they especially enjoyed waiting around while Mike was getting drum sounds though. Mike Flicker was great at incorporating their production ideas."

When production and mixing on *Dog and Butterfly* had wrapped, as happy as producer Mike Flicker recalled Heart being with the album, something was missing. "Upon completion, everybody but the group, meaning myself, the record company, the management, felt in a certain respect that when they said *Dog and Butterfly* was finished, that it lacked a single. It had a lot of good esoteric and musical qualities, but lacked a commercial hit. At that point, both myself and the manager knew their emotional investment into the album, and so we made a conscious decision not to say anything. Because, first, we felt it wasn't good for them: that they needed to deal with this themselves. So we went to the record company, and voiced our concerns, but told them we felt it wasn't our place to bring it to the girls, and turned them into the bad guys. But contractually, the record company could not do anything, they had to accept the record as is. But they could say something, so we got the head of Portrait, which was a division of CBS, to attend a listening party, then we all sat down and had dinner, and he said, 'We love what you got there, but think you're missing one song. That's our professional opinion.' And the girls took it the way I thought they would — which was not very well — but that then allowed the band to sit down and talk to us in a different way, and asked, 'Well, do you guys agree?' And in a sort of cowering way, we agreed, and basically from there, the band was given 10 days to produce another single. So it went from the girls, who then had a new writing partner in Sue Ennis, going away for a weekend, and coming back with 'Straight On,' and finishing the album. And if it wasn't for that single, I don't think the album would have done well."

Leese recalled the inspiration for the last-minute hit single, "We didn't add 'Straight On' till the very end because the label said we were missing a single. And at the time, Ann was listening to 'Grapevine' and 'Missing You,' by The Rolling Stones, which basically has the same groove, so that was the groove she wanted to use, and we all got together and tried to work something out. It was great for me because I come from a funk background." Co-writer Sue Ennis noted, "I came up with the concept and title for 'Straight On.' I was out on the road with them at the time, which I seldom did. I hardly traveled, because there wasn't much for me to do besides hang out, watch the band play, then give Ann and Nance constructive feedback about the shows. I remember waking up one morning, and thought, 'God, what if you had a song that was a big arrow aimed at somebody. Like I have to have you.' And I thought, 'How would you say that? I guess *straight on*, coming at you.' We built the song from the title really."

Describing the finished album's musical sophistication and maturity, *Rolling Stone* noted that "Nancy Wilson's guitar sets elegant counterpoint patterns against the melodies' deep purples and moody blues — her playing is as fresh and welcome as a lucid thought among the lyrics' free associations. There's a clarity to Ann Wilson's voice, a directness. She doesn't fool around much with tone or phrasing, she just gets louder and fiercer. It's not what she's singing, but the singing itself that gets to the point. Her voice slices through band member Howard Leese's beautiful, blowzy arrangements, saying: here, just here, this is where it hurts. It's this passionate precision and this precisely expressed passion that make both the boogie and ballads so persuasive." For Flicker, his favorite moments on the LP included

> 'We still feel quite proud of the album . . . the people who love it, love it deeply.'

"'Lighter Touch' because it was an interesting sound. It was played on an old Wurlitzer that one of them had at their house, and we had to bring that into the studio because it was really the whole sound of the song. It was something very funky. 'Dog and Butterfly,' I love that song, and the key to me on that was to try and make it musically and production-wise as simple as the story. I really fought my own mind, because it could have gone into a really big production. Finding the right instruments was important, and it turned out to be an original Wurlitzer, the electric piano sound we got. 'Mistral Wind' would probably be my favorite song on that album."

As for Nancy Wilson, "I guess one of the best Heart songs is 'Mistral Wind' from *Dog and Butterfly*. It's sort of an opus you know, sort of long winded, but it's got the poetry that matches the music. The music describes the lyrics really well and it takes you on a journey through a real crazy thing like life. But you come out the other side of it alive and wiser." Leese agreed, "To this day, I think 'Mistral Wind' is the best thing Heart ever did, from the subject matter to the epic nature of it, to the dissonance of the rifts, great drumming by Mike. Just the whole thing was a distillation of what Heart was about as a band — a real quiet, beautiful beginning, and then all hell breaks loose when that wind comes up, and Ann's voice shifts into rocket mode. When you're done listening to it you're like, 'Wow, I've been somewhere.' That album and the first one are the best of that first bunch of records in my opinion. Every song on *Dog and Butterfly* makes you go, 'Wow, that's pretty good.'"

Collaborator Sue Ennis was equally as proud of the LP, "Overall, I was thrilled with the album. Out of our collaborations on *Dog and Butterfly*, we developed a writing moniker of

Connie, which was Ann and Nancy and I. *Dog and Butterfly* is probably my favorite album just because that was a really great time in my life and in the life of our friendship. We still feel quite proud of the album. On the whole, the people who love it, love it deeply."

Upon release in September of 1978, *Dog and Butterfly* proved to be as much an exercise in commercial re-birth for Heart as it had been artistically, debuting in the top 20 of Billboard's Top 200 Album Chart, where it would remain for the next 36 weeks. The new album's success had a positive effect on the rest of the Heart catalog. "When we put out *Dog and Butterfly*, it dragged our first three albums back up the charts, so we had four albums in the Billboard Top 200," as Leese recalled. Producing hit singles with "Straight On" and "Dog and Butterfly," the album went double-platinum, and had critics as in love with the LP as Heart's fans were. Trying to recreate that critical and commercial success for its follow-up album in the midst of changing dynamics within the band, Heart began the writing and recording process for *Bebe Le Strange*.

CHAPTER 7

Bebe Le Strange

1980

Bebe Le Strange was an apt title for Heart's fifth studio LP; in an industry climate that focused narrowly on trends, the Wilsons went in another direction, seeking to be even freer from outside input than they had been on *Dog and Butterfly*. "The danger in the success of *Dog and Butterfly* probably came with our fifth album," guitarist Leese explained, "because we and our representatives were thinking, 'Wow, we can do no wrong,' which is dangerous thinking to fall into because you should never take any success for granted. Ann and Nancy were flexing their muscles a little bit more." Speaking for the Wilsons, Sue Ennis recalled that "heading into the next studio LP, *Bebe Le Strange*, Ann and Nance felt they had been making more of a contribution on the production front, and they didn't want to give Mike

> 'That was the end of an era — the '70s band was changing, and the decade was over.'

Flicker full producer power on that one. Also, I was much more involved on that album on both the writing and production. At the time Roger Fisher had left the band, and also, Ann broke up with Mike Fisher, so the Fisher brothers were out of the picture by that point. And they had been pretty controlling, and so I think without them, there was a sense that it was time to move on, and of a new strength and freedom on the girls' part in some ways. So their departure also prompted Ann and Nance to take the reins a little bit more in the studio."

Heading into writing for the album, producer Mike Flicker felt "there was a lot of searching in the music, which I think is dangerous, and I articulated [that] to the girls at the time. That album, I think I spent more time as a psychologist than as a producer, and it drove me away from the group. It was relationships, and all that came out musically, because it all becomes power structure." In zeroing in on where he felt the band came up weakest with this album, Leese cited what had arguably been their strongest point in previous efforts: songwriting. "On our fifth album, and final, working with producer Mike Flicker, *Bebe Le Strange*, I don't think Mike's authority was ever in question, he was always on top of every aspect of what we were doing in the studio, but on the writing side, the girls were stretching a little bit. If the album had any deficits, I think it was that the material wasn't as strong. And because we had maybe a bit of an air of invincibility because of how well *Dog and Butterfly* had done, there may have been a little bit of laziness in the writing, for whatever reason. That was the end of an era — the '70s band was changing, and the decade was over."

The 1970s wouldn't be the only thing to end by the completion and release of *Bebe Le Strange*; it would also be Heart's final collaborative chapter with Flicker, who had discovered the group and guided them sonically through their first wave of success over the course of five studio LPs. Flicker had sensed his time with the band was short even before work began on the group's fifth LP, explaining that "what was happening anyway on the album before [*Bebe Le Strange*] was everybody felt they could do it. So I think it was important for them to do that." This shifting tide caused the creative reins to slip out of Flicker's control behind the console. "You had Ann and Nancy, who are the driving force in the group, and then what influences them, and Nancy at that point was now dating the drummer, Michael Derosier, on and off, which became a problem in that all of a sudden, Michael decided he wanted to spread his creative wings, so all of a sudden there are new influences. And situations would come up where I'd get a phone call from Ann saying, 'I just sat down with Nancy, and she's got these crazy ideas, and I know they're coming from Michael. . . .' And they never would get directly confrontational with each other, which was the whole problem. Then at the same time, Ann's boyfriend was off doing the dirty with some other girls, and I get a phone call telling me I have to go tell this to Ann. So I was like, 'We're doing a record here!' I felt that album to be an album of compromises, because it would be, 'Okay, well if she gets to do this one, then we get to do this one, and if they get to do this one, we want our way on this one. . . .' So conceptually, that record became a reflection on the times, breaking into the '80s, the punk movement, and the upheaval in their personal lives."

Again Ann and Nancy enlisted Sue Ennis to aid with the writing of their fifth studio LP. "Nancy and Sue and I built a protective wall that we lived behind," explained Ann. "An exclusive society with its own language and its own culture." Nancy, for her part, explained that Ennis's "being a soulmate to both me and Ann had a lot to do with our joy of writing [with her]." From Leese's perspective, "Sue had a Ph.D. in literature, and was very literate and intelligent, so her input generally was lyrics. She would help the girls refine them and make them more elegant, coming up with the concept for the songs and how to put the prose together. She wasn't in the studio." Collaborating under the moniker *Connie*, the threesome moved from writing into producing, prompting Flicker to declare "the triumphant of Ann, Nancy and Sue Ennis. They nicknamed themselves a producer. They showed up a little more as a personality on that record, but the name was just their sense of humor. It was definitely production-by-committee, which was a negative because everything was a compromise. I would have left half the album off if I had my way."

Ann remarked to a journalist at the time, "It is rare to have a rock band 'fronted' by a woman, let alone find a band where two women are seen as the real creative force in making rock music. Girls were regularly sending us letters saying how they were inspired to learn guitar, or join a band, or dare to write rock songs because of us. Eventually, we began to see more and more of this reaction, and the idea for *Bebe Le Strange* emerged. It's a kind of collective name for all the young people who have contacted us; it's a name like Johnny B. Goode — it stands for much, much, more than a 'feminist statement' about rock. It goes beyond that. We are two women in a position rarely seen in rock. This album is meant as a dedication to and an acknowledgement of all those we've inspired."

Conceptually, Ennis explained that "*Bebe Le Strange* was inspired by a fan letter. We wrote that song from the perspective of a fan, sort of in love with a rockin' female character. I think there was a spirit of female liberation in that, although I don't want it to seem like it was in any way a women*centric* kind of album, it really wasn't. Of course, behind the scenes, there was a sense of 'Okay, now the power is where it really needs to be.' We still tended to want to do our little songwriting getaways. It seemed better when the three of us really got away so it wasn't like any of us had to go home and answer to people at the end of the day. The songwriting seemed to come out of those times with just the three of us, which went back to what we'd started as teenagers. And it was a great solace and feeling to know that that haven was still available to us as 30-year-olds. In some ways we were still teenagers in that place where we had our own language, our own private jokes. All of that was our own private little world that we could still conjure up. And that's where we could be most creative too.

"The writing process, which can be really hard sometimes, was so much fun for *Bebe* with the three of us together. Ann and Nance were contractually obligated to write an album, so why not make it a joyful experience that can also be familial and exhilarating, as opposed to writing with the band. The band guys really wanted to get in on the songwriting, so they would jam at sound check, come up with five minutes of a riff-rock type feel, hand it over, and say, 'Put a singing part on it.' And we'd say, sarcastically, 'A singing part? You mean write all the lyrics and the melodies, make the song actually say something and give it its entire character?' We never actually said that out loud, but it sure was a big joke with us. In those instances, we did write 'the singing part,' *and* the music part, and the lyrics. We felt considerable pressure from the band to include them [in the] writing so that they could get a piece of the royalties. This issue came up particularly when Mark and Denny joined the group [a few years later], because they were both established, and had certain expectations, which included being part of the writing. As I think back about *Bebe Le Strange*, I don't think there are a lot of 'band' songs on the record, but the seeds of that were planted there."

The big personnel change in the band had been on the horizon since the previous album; as Flicker noted, it was apparent in the virtual absence of original guitarist Roger Fisher from *Dog and Butterfly*. "If you listen to that album, there's very, very, very little Roger, compared to other albums, and that was sort of the beginning of the end for him, and during the production of that, the stuff that annoyed me about him began to annoy everybody. He, for a period, had also been Nancy's boyfriend, and so by this point, they had broken up, and he lost half of his protection that way. After that record, he was out. I think there was a point where . . . the confidence enough grew from the rest of the members, that his energy went from being an asset to being an annoyance. . . . He had been signed to the group because he was Ann's boyfriend's brother, it was that simple. Otherwise I never even would have signed him, because I didn't think he was a talented-enough musician. But I'm thankful I did, if only for those two riffs — they were a significant contribution. He was a pain in the ass in the studio, in life. He usually couldn't repeat the same thing twice in the studio, and he would frustrate himself to a certain extent. He had more in his brain than his fingers could do, so it got to a point where, if it came to a Roger guitar solo, after the first album, I left the room, because it became a three-day punching affair, almost note by note." Fisher, for his part, told a journalist that "once we got more famous, we lost sight of the need for greatness. It [became] . . . Ann and Nancy's band . . . not a group."

The impact of Fisher's absence was felt most heavily by lead guitarist Howard Leese. "I was still the main arranger for the band, but on that record, also became the full-time lead guitar player because Roger was gone, and another thing that made that album different was Nancy was playing a lot more electric guitar. It was fun for me because we had streamlined it a little bit, so there were five of us instead of six, which made things a little bit easier just overall with less people involved." For pro-

HOWARD LEESE   **MICHAEL DEROSIER**   **STEVE FOSSEN**
NANCY WILSON   **ANN WILSON**

MANAGEMENT
EN KINNEAR

) 241-2320

Heart's brand new line-up in 1980

ducer Mike Flicker, as ugly as most of his experience making the album was, he recalled one of his few enjoyable production moments as the recording of "'Silver Wheels,' which was Nancy's song, and came from her totally uninfluenced, which made it more enjoyable to track. Recording the Tower of Power horn section was an enjoyable experience. I used for close micing a lot of Ribbon microphones, old RCA 77s and 47s on that." The Wilson sisters also spread their instrumental wings on the LP, with Nancy playing Mellotron and piano, in addition to electric and acoustic

> 'Ann spoiled me, I never found anyone who could deliver the way she delivered.'

guitars, while Ann "is a singer first but also a great guitar, flute, piano, ukulele and bass player." Nancy also involved herself in the album's mixing, and shared some of her theories on the appropriate approach to EQing an LP as rock-heavy as *Bebe Le Strange*. "Usually if you flog a song by playing or singing it too many times, you can really wear it out, so we try and mix in a similar way, trying to stick to first instincts. . . . Perfection is the wrong road for rock 'n' roll. You can suck all the life out of it by fixing and improving a track out of existence until it's just too clean and tidy."

Unfortunately, everyone but Heart thought the album was just the opposite: a mess. So much so, that by the time the album had been completed, Flicker had also decided to wrap up his tenure with the band. The cumulative toll the making of *Bebe Le Strange* took on him made it "not a good experience for me. When we finished that album, my decision to part company with the band came from a combination of frustration and my feeling I had done as much as I could do with them. Pretty much after that album I said, 'I think the best thing you can do for your own musical, creative health is produce the next album yourself.' I think everybody needs to go through what they need to go through, so for me when they began to lose themselves in the songwriting, that was it. So there was no falling out, but it was apparent in *Bebe Le Strange* that everyone wanted to go in a different direction, and they didn't even know what that direction was. I stayed on good terms with the band. Post-Heart, after looking around some, I found that Ann spoiled me, I never found anyone who I felt could deliver the way she delivered, and I guess, to a certain extent, maybe I took that for granted while working with her. I just sort of assumed that there was more of that out there, and I never found it. She was irreplaceable, which made me feel soured and spoiled, and the industry itself was changing in a way that just wasn't fun for me anymore. So when it became a labor instead of a love, I had it and was over it."

The band was heading into uncharted territory, even for an veteran, multi-platinum rock act, and one of the first important allies they had lost in that fight critically was *Rolling Stone*, whose scathing review of the group's fifth album was so negative that it concluded that "the only excuse offered for Heart is that the notion of women playing hard rock is somehow liberating." Unfortunately, that card wouldn't save them from the backlash that would come with the album's release. Debuting at #5 on the Billboard Top 200 Album Chart, the album would spend 22 weeks on the chart, mostly in decline from the misleading first week showing. Ultimately, the album would sell only 500,000 copies, a far cry from the more than 2,000,000 units the band's last album had moved.

The underwhelming critical and commercial reaction to *Bebe Le Strange* would serve as the band's wake-up call, but one they were slow to heed, requiring one more colossal commercial bomb with the self-produced *Private Audition* LP, before Ann and Nancy Wilson agreed to explore other *Passionworks*.

CHAPTER 8

Private Audition
and *Passionworks*

1981–1983

Bebe Le Strange had been a failure for Heart commercially and critically. Before returning to the studio, the band issued a live album to tide fans and critics over, but didn't make up much ground with the latter group at least, with *Rolling Stone* saying the album "kicks off well . . . and promptly falls apart." This criticism came from the mothership of all mainstream rock critics, which was keeping it real with Heart in a time when its management and record label were not. Perhaps the magazine, which historically had been a great champion of the band's cause for female competition in male-dominated rock 'n' roll, was trying to constructively criticize a band it loved too much not to? Whether or not this tough-love criticism influenced the direction Ann and Nancy Wilson took the band with 1982's

> '. . . when Mike left, it was hard for me because I had known Mike a lot longer than the band.'

self-produced *Private Audition*, by the conclusion of its recording, Heart had gone a long way to winning back the love of their most prominent and influential critics among record buyers. With *Private Audition*, Heart made it clear that it was still fighting for credibility and against artistic compromise, at a time when the latter was on the rise. Ann Wilson explained to a journalist years later that "the '80s was a really successful time for Heart, but also very stressful. That was an artificial period for pop culture. I don't know of another time when such a low value was placed on naturalness. We were really stressed out because you know, that's really not us."

Heart initially enlisted one of the industry's top producers, Jimmy Iovine, who had just come off producing John Lennon's *Double Fantasy* LP, to replace departed producer Mike Flicker. Flicker's absence was hardest personally on guitarist Howard Leese. "After *Bebe Le Strange*, when Mike left the fold as producer, it was hard for me because I had known Mike a lot longer than the band. He and I had started the label together, and were a successful team before we did Heart. I felt more loyalty to him, and if he would have asked me to leave, I probably would have, but by then I'd been in the band a long time, and had done a lot of work, and had loyalties there as well, and was enjoying being in the band. When I first joined Heart, I didn't know I would be in the band for more than 20 years. But by the time Mike left, I don't know if he actually came to me and said, 'I'm leaving, but don't let it affect you,' but that was the feeling I got. It wasn't a big 'You're fired' or 'We're done,' it just sort of fizzled out. There was quite a break between *Bebe Le Strange* and our next recording, which I think was a live album. . . . The next record we did was *Private Audition*, which we made in 1981. When we started that record, Jimmy Iovine was producing, and his engineer was a guy named Shelly Yatkins. So we started making the record, and had tracked maybe eight, nine, ten songs, then Jimmy called us in

and said, 'The stuff is great, you guys sound great, but I don't hear any hits. I don't hear any singles; I don't think we have a hit for this record.' Next thing you know, he's gone. I don't know if he quit, or if the girls fired him, but now me and the girls are producing the record by ourselves. . . . Shelly Yatkins stayed to help us engineer and finish the thing."

According to Sue Ennis, the Wilsons decision to self-produce the LP stemmed both from Flicker's departure and the sisters' experience as co-producers of the previous album. "When Mike Flicker decided to leave following *Bebe Le Strange* and prior to *Private Audition*, I think that everyone was at the end of the road, but it wasn't acrimonious at all. Ann and Nance were just feeling more confident in the studio, almost like, 'Why should we have somebody tell us what to do, even if it's Flicker?' During production, I was in the studio with the team for every performance, and there really was teamwork, so I would say I was as involved both in the writing and production as well, for the first time really. (Yes, on what would become the least successful of Heart records.) Howard Leese stayed with the band after Mike Flicker left, and was a big help during the production with engineering, in addition to everything else he already did within Heart. He had great musical chops, and wrote string charts for *Dog and Butterfly*, and conducted those sessions with the orchestra, and, of course, Howie is a fantastic guitar player. Of all the people in the band, he was the one guy who had the technical side down, he could read music and knew theory. So those were the main things that made him an asset, because Ann and Nancy played more by ear. They learned to read music over the years, and if you put Nance in front of a piece of music right now, she would work her way through it, but none of us had near the level of expertise that Howard had."

The band proceeded, throwing out much of what they had tracked with Iovine and starting over from scratch. Leese reflected on the approach: "The way the girls worked was when things are going badly, they will listen to people's advice and will defer a little bit of control to other people — management or other songwriters. But when things are going great, they say, 'We can do this ourselves, we don't need these guys.' So that was our first lesson in that. The girls wrested total control of that record, and it ended up not being a very good record and not doing well at all. It was our only record not to sell gold or platinum, because they wouldn't listen to anybody. People tried to tell them, and they wouldn't listen, and had to learn the hard way."

In spite of the pressure, Ennis explained that the production trio of *Connie* (she, Ann and Nancy) kept an upbeat vibe. "When Ann and Nancy were recording their instrumental and vocal parts, we were all present for every session, and we would do our little quotes from Beatles' things like this one George Harrison clip on the end of 'Piggies' on the *White Album*, where he said, 'One more time.' So if we were doing any one of their vocal sessions, and something needed to be sung again, we'd say in this British accent, 'One more time.' Just little familiar things like that to keep it light. We always kept it light."

The band's sixth studio LP in six years fared poorly with fans upon its release, something Leese thought resulted from the lack of outside influence on the record and its disconnect with the '80s music world. "We did a nice job on the record sonically; the material was the weakest part. The producer tried to tell us that, and we wouldn't listen, and if we'd had one, we probably would have kept writing or come up with some other songs. Musically

it's a fine record, I like listening to it, but it doesn't have a
catchy single. And by then,
there was more emphasis on
singles and videos than the
whole overall scope of a
record. Being out of the '70s,
we weren't dealing with album

'. . . that album was our

first case of having too

much control.'

radio anymore, now it was MTV, and your first song and first
video better be great, or else the whole thing could fall apart. So
that album was our first case of having too much control and
not knowing what to do with it."

Sue Ennis further reflected that "when we were writing
Private Audition, we were feeling kind of mighty. We also felt
like, 'Let's try to write something that isn't necessarily commercial, let's experiment and explore some things that we want to
do. Make it like a variety show, all kinds of styles that we like,
and here's some little moments of thoughtful reflection of
maybe the politics of the time,' all these things. And there's no
doubt that we were thinking like, 'Remember *Sgt. Pepper*, they
just wrote the songs, and somehow it all worked together.' I
think we sincerely thought that somehow it would find a place
with fans. There was never a question of 'Do you think this
isn't going to reach an audience?' So the writing and recording
of that album was great fun, but the footnote to that was that
we weren't quite as close because Nance was off pursuing a
relationship. She was very caught up in that. She wasn't really
quite with us, and it was just one of those things that relationships do sometimes, so we were kind of scattered as a writing
team during that album."

Though *Private Audition* peaked in the Billboard Album
Chart's Top 40 at a respectable 25 in May 1982, it was a far cry
from their first four albums' performances, and more akin to the
downward trend that had begun with *Bebe Le Strange*. Still, the

album would spend 15 weeks on the chart and produced a moderately successful single with "This Man Is Mine," earning one of its most valuable critical allies back with *Rolling Stone*, which warmly concluded that "the successes outweigh the embarrassments, making *Private Audition* Heart's bravest LP to date."

"When the album came out and didn't do well, we were super-disappointed of course," Ennis recollected. "But then, over time, you revisit the songs, and looking back now, I think it was sort of an indulgent album. Luckily it wasn't the nail in the career coffin, which it could have been because it really did not sell well. I think some of the songs had potential, but we didn't stick with them long enough. We didn't edit them, and didn't get in and work on them hard enough to develop them into something that would make sense to listeners. But the album did reflect what was happening at that time in our lives, particularly with relationships. It was a drifty, unfocused time. Still, in spite of that, the three of us remained solid. Nance returned to the *Connie* fold, and we moved forward. No doubt behind our backs, people were saying, 'Sue is the reason the album didn't work.' People are eager to blame someone for a failure. But it was simplistic. Because I was just one team member. However, when things got shaky and scary there, I became a bit of a scapegoat. It was never said to my face, but I could feel it, although *never* from Ann or Nancy. So when it came time for our next LP, *Passionworks*, the three of us were still joined at the hip as the writing team."

Heart's record sales spoke a bleak message to the band, one its label made loud and clear for the group's next LP, *Passionworks*: Epic Records insisted they work with a producer. Even prior to the label's decision, Ann and Nancy Wilson had already been busy with inner-band housekeeping — throwing out half of its foundation. As guitarist Howard Leese, who the sisters tasked with re-forming Heart's backing player line-up, recalled, "What

'The band is broken and we want you to fix it.'

had started going on was Steve Fossen and Mike Derosier had started their own side group, which I think really bothered the girls. So after we finished promoting *Private Audition*, Steve and Mike were fired, and Steve and Roger had started the band, so it was hard for them. What happened was, Ann called me one day and said, 'The band is broken and we want you to fix it. We want you to pick the new guys.' So in a way, that was really great for me, because now here I have some real control, and could put a new band together and really kick some serious ass. Ann and Nancy had given me a huge responsibility, and so now suddenly I was the senior guy, and that was the point at which I assumed that overall kind of role as musical director in the band. I needed a new drummer and bass player, and wanted to get the best players possible. I knew right off the bat who I wanted for drums; I had previously done a record with Denny Carmassi and Mike Flicker — a Randy Misner record before Heart. And I'd told him when things had started to go bad on the last album, 'I can smell the winds of change; don't be surprised one day if I call you.' So once I got him, then for bass player, I auditioned a number of guys. Mark Andes was really my first choice, and so I gave him a call, he came over and played for me, and I pretty much knew these guys would be perfect. They'd never met, they met for the first time at the airport in Seattle when they flew in, and I put them into the band and the girls loved them and off we went. The first thing we wanted to do was make a new record, so we all went into the studio in L.A. and started making *Passionworks*."

The new band members were soon joined by a new producer. As Ennis explained, "Heading into *Passionworks*, the decision to team up with an established producer was a foregone conclusion. The label demanded it, and Ann and Nance got along well with

Keith Olsen at the mixing board with Ann's dog

Keith [Olsen], and because Denny and Mark had joined the band on drums and bass as a new rhythm section, there was a new feeling all around. Keith and Denny had also worked together before, so they talked up making the album work by presenting the sense of a strong, unified band. The concept of the band — certainly among members — had become important again, and as a result, there was a shift in the vibe of Heart, which coincided with meeting Keith. So it was a new era they were ready to explore."

Keith Olsen, the man who Heart's record label enlisted to produce their seventh LP, was one of the hottest producers in pop rock at the time, known within the industry as the "Air Hawk" for all the radio time his productions were receiving at the time, including Rick Springfield's "Jessie's Girl," "Hit Me With Your Best Shot" by Pat Benatar, among other #1 smashes. A

bedrock of Olsen's multi-platinum production philosophy resonated with the Wilsons' approach to music: "Part of my main
role as a producer is picking and shaping a great song into a hit.
The thing is you get a feeling when you're working with songs,
because they impart a really good story. 'I'm Winning' with
Santana, who hadn't had a hit in 15 years till that song. The opening lines of that song, I could relate to that, and the approach to
recording that great song is what makes it more listenable, but if
the story nails your listener, it doesn't really matter, all this crap
about sample rates, or this mic or that mic. It is all about great
songs, followed by that great performance."

Heading into the writing for *Passionworks*, the underwhelming commercial response to *Private Audition* weighed heavily on
Ann and Nancy Wilson. Sue Ennis explained that "*Private
Audition*'s failure to find an audience was a punch in the gut; we
were certainly more self-conscious in writing the next record.
We had to think about certain things in the context of songwriting that we hadn't had to think about in a year and a half, like,
well, reaching an audience. We had a big-time producer, so they
definitely felt 'the thrust of the album is to try to get back what
we've lost, and discover a new audience.' And the album was
aimed at finding some radio play, so when Keith brought in
'Allies' from outside writers, I think it was like, 'Well, this is the
pill we have to swallow.' Ann and Nance's reaction was not 'we
love the song,' it was more what the manager was saying, 'Time
to leave it to the experts who are gonna get you back out there.
Let's steady the boat a little bit, we've gotten wobbly. And part of
what needs to happen is to cover this song.'"

Olsen's greatest challenge, as had been Iovine's, was selling
the Wilson sisters on the idea of recording material written outside the band for the sake of a hit to sell the album. Though he
was eventually successful, it proved a considerable challenge, one
that, guitarist Howard Leese recalled, began with "looking at it as
the first record of the '80s band, then it makes a little bit more

'. . . it wouldn't break anything if someone else wrote some songs.'

sense. On any first record for a new band, there are going to be growing pains feeling each other out, looking for a sound and for your identity, and you're trying to gel. In a different way also, that record was an important record for us because we had all the songs, and had started cutting the songs, and once we had most of the material laid out, we had the same meeting we'd had with Jimmy Iovine, where Keith said, 'I'd really like to bring in an outside song.' And the girls wouldn't hear it, didn't want to know about it, wouldn't listen to him, wanted to write all the stuff themselves, which was a really important issue for them. So Keith said, 'I have this one song by Jonathan Kane from Journey called 'Allies'; it's a perfect song for you guys.' So he brings in the song, plays it for us, and we said, 'That's actually a pretty great song. Ann will sing the crap out of that.' So the key to that record and for our success to come is Keith Olsen convincing Ann and Nancy that it wouldn't break anything if someone else wrote some songs. No one's going to care, no one's going to know, it's still going to say 'Heart,' it's not that big of a deal. So when we recorded 'Allies,' that was a big turning point. So Keith broke the ice with that song, and *Passionworks* had some good stuff on it, so I felt like we were on our way back up. We had a new manager, a new record label and a new producer."

Olsen explained how he recorded the bed tracks for *Passionworks*: "I tracked drums, bass and one guitar, and Nancy would usually put her guitar parts on afterward. Howard had really good time, and Denny Carmassi had really great time, and the bass player, he and Carmassi together were incredible." Olsen felt Nancy's primary strength in the studio was her "vocals, she can sing with Ann really well, and it's that sibling sound, and sounds fabulous. Another of her important strengths was she was an *adequate* guitar player, and when I say adequate, that means she played in tune and in time. Is she one of those great players? No. But was she adequate, absolutely, and very definitely a key woman in that band." When attention turned to tracking Ann Wilson's (by this time legendary) rock voice, Olsen found it to be the least challenging step in recording the album, simply because "Ann Wilson is an example of just a world-class singer. I've been very lucky to have worked with a number of world-class singers, and I put her right in that batch. Every time she opens her mouth, it sounds incredible. There's this really weird song on that record called 'Johnny Moon,' where the vocal performance is spectacular."

Revealing how he adapted to Ann's truly outside-the-box approach to tracking the album's vocals, Olsen recalled, "What Ann liked to do when she was recording vocals was walk around the studio. If you made her stand in one place and sing on a microphone, her vocal performance would stiffen. So I said, 'Okay, well how do you do it live?' And she said, 'Well, I hand-hold a mic.' So I said, 'Okay, hand-hold this,' and gave her a 451 with a piece of foam rubber tie-wrapped around the whole thing, so it was like a shock absorber, and then put a little wind-screen on the tip, and handed her headphones with a headphone box with a belt-clip on it, and she just lapped around the studio, prancing back and forth, screaming out all those songs." In spite of their unique vocal recording apparatus, Olsen explained that "I always make sure I control it, because the worst thing you can ever possibly do is stick a mic out in a room that's empty with headphones, and say, 'Go out there and sing.' The most important part of any song is the lead vocal because it's the melody and the story and the performance, right there, all in one thing. So every lead singer's really self-critical and very concerned about it, and it's the hardest thing to do. So at all times, I also tried to keep the people in the control room down to just the people who are necessary." For Ann, that meant Howard Leese and her sister

Nancy with her studio
companions

Nancy, who proudly felt that "every producer,
including me, has been blown completely away.
There is only one Ann Wilson."

Olsen was in ready agreement with Nancy; Ann's seemingly
effortless process for tracking vocals was a truly magical one for
him where within "four takes we would have every single vocal,
within four takes! I record warm-up vocals as a rule, but with
Ann, she was always spot-on." Olsen found it just as much a
pleasure recording Ann and Nancy Wilson's harmonies for the

album, recalling that "it was easy blending her and Ann's vocals because they're siblings, so there's that similarity of timbre. So it just blends. It's so easy it doesn't matter if it's loud or soft, it just works, because you aren't trying to synthesize a blend, it just happens. It's a natural phenomenon. We would do the lead vocals first, and then we'd do a couple of parts in backgrounds, and sometimes Nancy would sing alone, and sometimes Ann would join with her, and made them really strong. But there again, everything is at the same exact timbre, the same family of sinus cavity size, or whatever it is that made it a really easy blend."

For the album's crunchy rock guitars, Olsen deferred to the same approach that had scored Rick Springfield a hit, explaining that "the guitar on the intro to the record I made before the Heart record, 'Jessie's Girl,' by Rick Springfield, is a Dean Mockley guitar into my Suber amp. I had these amps that Jim Marshall made for me personally, with two EVN ML12s and an open back cabinet that weighed about 100 pounds, with a 100-watt head built into this little combo-cabinet. And it would rattle the tubes like crazy, and so any time you crunch on the guitar, the chunk would be brilliant and so strong, and the delayed chord that came after it. The poor tubes were just being hammered, because the sound pressure level inside that cabinet where those tubes were sitting was 135-decibel sound pressure level. So it added quite a lot to the sound. We used 57 and 451 mics with -10 on the cabinets, and ran them straight into the board."

Leese noted the contrasts in Olsen's production style with Heart veteran Mike Flicker. "On the technical side, every producer has their own style of working, so Mike Flicker's records sounded a certain way because of that. Mike was the most sensitive to the girls' material. They were writing really strong material in the early days, and Mike was really good at going through their songs and distilling it down to songs that were going to translate onto the record. I think he was almost like a member of the group. He was in the trenches with us every day working on the different parts of the songs, really, really getting his hands dirty working on the arrangements. Keith Olsen was waiting more for us to have it together already. He had his own studio, and therein his own style of working, but didn't get in the trenches with us quite as much to work on every little detail of the song. He was more about recording the songs, and overseeing the whole thing, but he didn't seem as much a member of the group. But I loved working with him, because he was a very creative guy and funny guy, and it was fun making that record."

Upon completion, hopes among the members of Heart were high for the new LP, but Leese recalled it was tempered by a healthy dose of humility. "You could tell as we finished that record and went out to play live the first few times that the new band was gonna be great. I could tell it was gonna work, and it was interesting because at that time, we weren't as famous. We weren't playing stadiums anymore, we were still playing arenas, but I remember on that tour, we had John Cougar Mellencamp opening for us, and a couple months into the tour, he had two singles in the Top 10. It was great for the shows because he brought people in, and here our opening act is bigger than we are. So that was a little bit uncomfortable for some of us, but was great in terms of new fans. At the end of that tour, 'How Can I Refuse?' was doing pretty well as a video on MTV, and that song had been written by the whole band, so we felt if we stuck with the formula of writing some of our own stuff, but being open to other songs, it would be a good balance." *Passionworks* was more in line with the times stylistically, and Heart began their long climb back to the top of the charts, debuting in the Top 40 (albeit at #39) of Billboard's Top 200 Album Chart in August 1983. Coupled with the singles-chart success of "Allies" and "How Can I Refuse?," the band had also further impressed their biggest and toughest critic, *Rolling Stone*, which hailed *Passionworks* for "showcas[ing] Ann Wilson's vocal pyrotechnics. . . . The most insistent Heart fan will find much to cheer about here."

Though it would sell 500,000 units and eventually go platinum, *Passionworks* was only one step up the ladder Heart was climbing to the top of rock stardom. With the business of pop music focused on selling artists on their image rather than on the strength of their sound, Heart still had a long way to go. Surviving that journey as the 1980s rolled on would force the band to get into bed with everything they had stood against in the 1970s, from marketing their sexuality in music videos to working with outside writers for virtually all of their hit singles. In spite of the fact that those concessions soon returned Heart to the upper tiers of the commercial '80s rock arena, Ann Wilson told a journalist years later that the compromises "offended us actually. . . . What happened was — and I don't want to lay the blame on MTV — but when we first started the band it was a radio thing, it was an audio thing. Suddenly here comes MTV where it's visual. People can't just listen to the music and have their own imagination and take them where they wanna go. You have to also provide a video for it, look a certain way and big hair. . . . If you're a woman it's even more strange with fake fingernails and corsets and all this stuff that was big in the '80s. At first it was fun. It was like theatre, it was like Queen or something, all theatrical. Then after a little while we went like, 'Fuck this man, this is just . . . piss off with this!' Seventies into the '80s was fun at first but then it got really boring." Veterans of reinvention by this point in their almost decade-long career, Ann and Nancy, as Howard Leese accurately put it, "had learned a couple of good tricks, as things went along," and would put them to use as they worked on their self-titled comeback LP.

CHAPTER 9

Heart and *Bad Animals*

1984–1988

By 1984, Heart's career — commercially speaking — was in need of a massive kick-start. In spite of the modest radio hits that the *Passionworks* LP had produced in 1983 with the singles "Allies" and "How Can I Refuse?," Epic Records still opted to drop the band from its artist roster in 1984. Capitol picked up Heart and the label change turned out to be just what the band needed.

The strings that came attached to Heart's new record deal included legendary pop rock producer Ron Nevison, who would go on to produce the band exclusively over their next two albums. "In the fall of 1984," recalled Nevison, "I got a call from my manager, Michael Lippman, who also represented Bernie Taupin, Elton John's lyricist, and George Michael among others. He asked me, 'What do you think about Heart?' And I said, 'Man,

I love them! Are you kidding, they're one of my favorite bands. I think Ann is incredible, I've always loved them.' And he says, 'Well, Don Grierson has just signed them at Capitol Records, and they want to talk to you about doing a couple of their ballads.' And my ambition was to do a full album, because with an artist who had been as big as them, they had the potential to be so again. What had happened, as you know, was that Heart had come out with one of the biggest debut albums of the '70s. I think, except for Boston, Heart had one of the biggest debuts of that decade. And I had always thought, when I first heard them, that this is a cool rock 'n' roll band — a girl with lungs like this and moves like that — that had both sides. The key elements for rock in those days were to have the rockers and the ballads; it was critical. It happened with all the hits I had, even Bad Company. So by the early 1980s, Heart had become a little fluff band and had strayed from that formula. And while Heart was really adept at the *Dog and Butterfly* type stuff, they really weren't rocking; they had lost that side of them. And their sales, they had lost their lead single potential, so by 1984 Epic had dropped them. But Don Grierson had seen their potential, and had taken a chance and signed them, but with a warning that there had been some conditions to their record deal. Basically, Don had said, 'I will sign you if you agree to two things: one, that we will mutually agree on the producer, and two, we will mutually agree on the songs, and that includes material from outside writers if necessary.' And they'd agreed, which Heart had never done before. That also would have been a condition of mine in working with them, but it never came up because Don took care of it."

Sue Ennis explained, "Don Grierson at Capitol Records is the one who plucked them back up, because he was personally a huge fan of Ann's voice. He believed in her. In fact, I believe in the beginning he only wanted to sign Ann, but subsequently after some meetings and he understood what the band dynamic was, and then said, 'Yes, this is Heart.' But he laid the vision of

Heart with Capitol Records president Don Grierson and legendary producer Ron Nevison

what the album would be. He brought Ron Nevison on board, who brought in an Austrian musician Peter Wolf, who was a gifted arranger. So under Grierson's guidance a handpicked team was brought in. I think the deal was we're gonna sign you but we're gonna do it our way. At that point the band had also switched management to Howard Kaufman's firm. Feisty, diminutive Trudy Green was their personal manager, but she was still part of the team at Kaufman's company who were figuring out the marketing of the band, the look of the band, the videos. A big machine was starting to crank up on behalf of Heart, and I think Ann and Nancy felt conflicted about it. On one hand, they were happy to be back among the wanted, but as the process went on, and it became clear that a lot of the decisions were being made about how to market them were being made by others. The decision to emphasize Nance in the videos, for example. Trudy Green was a hard-driving, persuasive manager, who basically said, 'You guys, we're gonna get on this train, and ride it back to the top and here's how we're going to do it.' So when Ann and Nance said, 'Okay,' I think they were somewhat naïve."

Heart was finally open to recording songs written outside the band, a move they had long resisted. This willingness reflected their awareness of what was at stake — their future commercial viability. Nancy conceded to a journalist at the time, "We never wanted to but there was a time when it looked like we faced an abyss. It's just a real big budget lifestyle because there's just so many people involved. And making the album, we paid for that, we paid for the videos. We have the best crew around, as far as I'm concerned, and we'd never let them go. That's expensive, especially when you're not on the road. You know, it's just as easy to lose it all really fast as it is to make it really fast. . . . Basically, we had all of our chips on the *Heart* album. If that didn't do something, then we were probably going to have to do something else; we would have been forced to." Sue Ennis also noted, "As far as the large repertoire of out-side-penned singles goes, Ann had sung her share of cover tunes over the years in bar bands, so she could tackle any song, throw herself into it and make it her own. Also, it was pretty clear by that time that the *machine* didn't want our songs anymore. They threw us a bone with a couple of what they deemed 'filler tracks.' That's how we felt about it anyway, but it was clear the management and label had a vision about what the hit songs needed to be. And what that sound needed to be, which is where Ron Nevison entered the picture." Longtime lead guitarist Howard Leese recalled, "When we left Epic in 1984 and signed with Capitol, the band hadn't been doing that well, so we kind of knew this was really going to be our last big shot. If this record tanked, we might not have a record deal, and when things weren't going well, the girls tended to be a lot more interested in listening to other people's ideas and opinions."

On the basis of that understanding, Nevison had an initial meeting with the Wilsons. "I wanted to see what they were interested in, so they flew me up to Seattle, and I had dinner with Ann, and we talked and we talked and we talked. She was telling me how much she liked the records I had produced, and I was telling her how she was one of my favorite singers. It was a meeting to feel each other out, so we didn't talk about anything specific to the album at that point. I remember she drove me back to the Four Seasons in her Porsche. And before I left I met again with Ann and Nancy together, which was equally as positive. I think part of what initially drew them to me might have been that they were *huge* Led Zeppelin fans, and I had engineered the *Physical Graffiti* album, and I think they were very impressed that I could do that and also have hits with poppier artists. I had 12 years in the game already, with lots of major records including The Who, Bad Company, Jefferson Starship and so forth. So the collective of those things worked in my favor. So within a few days of getting back to L.A., their manager called mine and said, 'The girls have been talking, and they'd like Ron to do the entire album.' And this was before we'd ever stepped into the studio together. I think initially they'd wanted to have several producers — I didn't ask and still don't know — but they just thought we had clicked."

Once Nevison and the Wilsons had planted the roots of their creative chemistry, they headed into pre-production, as the producer recalled, in high spirits. "By the time I got a call about formally working with them, Ann and Nancy had a new manager, Trudy Green. And though I think were a little bit hurt that Epic Records had dropped them after so long; at the same time,

'For the first time in a few years, everybody believed in them.'

they felt energized by the new regime of a new label, new manager and now the prospect of a new producer. For the first time in a few years, everybody believed in them, so their spirits were high, and on the whole, they had a good foundation. So I do think I had them at the right time." The band wasted no time on their comeback album, with Nevison first turning his attention to rounding up the album's hits. Leese explained, "Heading into the *Heart* record, Ron Nevison had been paying attention and had seen what Jimmy Iovine and Keith had gone through, and the results, and a key clause of the whole deal with him producing us was his saying, 'There's a lot of talent here, but I need authority, I need to be able to say no, these songs aren't good enough.' And he was right."

"My typical approach to pre-production when working with a band, obviously before we started rehearsals, I would be familiar with their music," detailed Nevison. "And I would have had a meeting with the band — as I did with Ann, and then with both Ann and Nancy. Then I would listen to the demos, and tell them what I thought of the music, whether I thought they had what they needed in the way of songs, and if they didn't, I would tell them to go back and write more stuff. Or find songs for them, depending on the situation. The latter is how it went with Heart. And in song terms, that could be a single, or a follow-up single. So when I first heard Heart's self-penned demos for the album, while I did think they had a lot of great material, I just wasn't sure about the singles. I had first listened to see what they had, and what was missing, and then started filling in the gaps. I didn't just go out and find songs for them, until I determined what they had. And I liked all their songs, but they needed some solid single material. And I had a mandate from their record label to do so. I wanted them to know that when we made a choice, it was a choice we were all making. It wasn't just my choice. I wanted them to know that if I wanted them to do 'Alone' or 'What About Love,' that Don Grierson wanted them to do that song, that the managers wanted them to do that song, along with me. So I had the backing of everybody."

While Nevison might have had the backing of Heart's representatives and the band in principle, the initial process

> '. . . if you can't make it your own, I'm not going to make you do it.'

of selling the Wilsons on several of the outside singles proved to be a challenging one. Beginning with the album's first single, "What About Love," Nevison recalled that "that song was written by Jim Vallance, and was given to me by Capitol Records President Don Grierson. I remember specifically being up at Nancy's house in Snohomish, Washington, rehearsing, and when I played that song, Nancy left the room. She wasn't happy with that song at first for Heart. They hated the treatment and production of the demo, and I think it was more the vocal they hated. Because the vocal in the demo was so wimpy, and I said, 'Listen, here's the way it's gonna be: I am not going to force you to do any song. But also, when you listen to a demo, I don't want you to listen to somebody's wimped-out vocal, because you guys are the greatest singers in the entire fuckin' rock world. So I want you to think of this demo as musical notes on paper. Pretend I handed you a lyric and music sheet, and you're gonna play it as a band, and if you can't make it your own, I'm not going to make you do it.' And suddenly, it came alive, and there was a lesson there. A producer can listen through and past that. I was only listening to melodies and notes, not to vocal performances and production. A lot of people aren't capable of seeing past that, but Don Grierson was and I was, and I didn't have to make Heart do it. They started playing it, and once Ann and Nancy heard it on tape, they went 'Oh . . . okay.' It became much more their song by the time we'd gone from pre-production to proper recording. I'll never forget the day that their managers came into the studio,

Howard Leese
Denny Carmassi   Ann Wilson
Mark Andes   Nancy Wilson

HEART

Management:
FRONT LINE/
TRUDY GREEN
(818) 777-6000

Capitol
RECORDS

right after I cut the basic track at the Record Plant in L.A., which was just a rhythm guitar, keyboard and vocal on it. They flipped out over it, and the girls were almost over the moon, everybody was, at how good it had turned out. And I hadn't even mixed it yet. So the lesson there is always jump to conclusions slowly."

Another of the album's eventual singles, which Nevison had a much easier time selling the band on, was "If Looks Could Kill." The producer felt instinctively the song would be a perfect follow-up to "What About Love." "I'm of the opinion that if you want to do something that's a ballad, that's great, but if it's gonna have any pace at all, it's gotta rock. 'If Looks Could Kill' is one example of a song that I got a hold of and rocked it up. That song originally was sitting on Don Grierson's desk headed for Tina Turner, and I grabbed it first and turned it into a very cool Heart song. I thought it would be perfect for Ann lyrically, especially the chorus, and it was. She tore that up. 'Nothing At All' proved to be another hit single. It had a catchy chorus that was perfect for Ann as well." Nevison also changed the performance dynamic of the band, a significant departure from Heart's norm for the better part of a decade. Up to that point, Nevison explained, "there had been a tradition that Nancy only sang one song on each album, and I thought, 'Well, in the off chance that Nancy had a hit, I wouldn't be able to follow that up.' On a 12-song album, why shouldn't she do two? I created that precedent. I thought she had way too good a voice to just do one song. That was one of the first things I thought would be important to the project."

The song that had first caught Nevison's ear as perfectly tailored to Nancy's voice turned out to be the album's third — and biggest — single, "These Dreams." It had first landed in his hands by "working with Michael Lippman, who was my manager, but also managed Bernie Taupin, Elton John's lyricist. As a result, we got some great songs from Bernie for the Heart albums. I had probably gone up to Seattle three or four times before we started cutting the album for rehearsals, and as I was headed up for one of those rehearsals, before I'd left, Bernie had handed me this tape with four or five songs he'd written with different guys. Humorously, one of them was 'We Built This City (On Rock 'n' Roll),' and I went, 'No fucking way, I am not going to stoop that low with this band.' But there was another one called 'These Dreams,' which I thought would be great for Nancy, because she's sort of a space cadet in a nice way, and the song was dreamy. So I thought it would be perfect for her. I was listening lyrically and image-wise, and that's why 'We Built This City' wouldn't have worked, but 'These Dreams' was an obvious choice for Nancy. I had heard it on the plane for the first time, got off and went and played it for them. When I had first played the demo, I played it in front of both sisters, and had prefaced it by saying, 'I found a song for Nancy.' Ann objected a little to that at first, but she never confronted me directly about any objections or issues she might have had, she went to her manager Trudy Green, who would then communicate them to me, and we'd hash it out. We didn't have that kind of overly personal rapport or routine, it all stayed very professional. So if either of the girls had an issue with something during the making of the album, she'd call Trudy, [who] would call me. When I had to make a point, I got support from their managers and the record label. So in the end, Ann was a team player and went along with it."

Nevison and the band settled on the album's final track list, and got into a pre-production routine. "Once we'd gathered all the material," recalled Nevison, "we got together and rehearsed it up in Seattle at Nancy's house, and worked on maybe three or four songs a day. And we just got them to the point where they were ready to be recorded, figuring tempo out, things like that. A lot of times, the endings and intros would need to be worked on, and sometimes I would have to rearrange the entire song from its original demo with the band. With Heart, I knew we had a good team, so I would send them the songs ahead of time, and once they got familiar, then I'd come up to hear what they'd done and make notes. So by the time we went in to record, Heart knew all the arrangements of the songs, and everyone knew their parts perfectly."

Legendary for running a tight ship with an all-business attitude in the studio, producer Ron Nevison explained, "With Heart, as with every other act I produced, I tried to avoid anything non-musical. I think if you get too close as a member of the band while you're trying also to be producer, you can't accomplish a lot of the things you need to: you can't spank them when you need to, verbally. You have to be able to — not rule with an iron hand, I don't want to be misconstrued — but you have to be able to accomplish your goals. And sometimes, in order to be a taskmaster, you have to put your foot down. I never looked at myself as being difficult, but I'm demanding. I demand a lot from my artists, and I think they would want that. You have to understand that it's a very difficult juggling act that you have to perform when you're a producer in a situation like this. When I had to, I was their pal, and when I couldn't, I wouldn't." Ennis explained the effect that approach had on Ann, "As opposed to Mike Flicker's great finesse, Ron Nevison was the producer who didn't give the soft touch in his feedback. So I think Ann suffered from that. She was a little tender about not being treated with kid gloves, and not for her ego. She always sang the best when she knew that behind the glass, there was a bunch of people wishing her well. And Ron — good for him — was hell bent on pulling the performances out of her that would make a hit record. So his heart was in the right place, and he was hired to do the job he did, and did it really well. But I wouldn't say it was a super-pleasant creative atmosphere."

Nevison's discipline in the studio, according to Leese, allowed Heart to work at a highly productive pace which, from the guitarist's perspective, made "those records surprisingly easy to do, especially cutting the basic tracks. Denny's such a great drummer. He would rehearse ahead of time, working out all the drum and bass patterns with Mark Andes, and we'd have vocal rehearsals. With a lot of those singles that were penned by other writers outside the band, we'd learn them quickly, lay them down and move on. We were tracking 30 songs in all, and recording two tracks in one day. For instance, with the single 'Nothing at All,' we learned that song in the morning, and tracked it that afternoon. We also had a great advantage in having two *ridiculous* engineers on that record. On the first record we did with Ron, we also had Mike Clink as the engineer, which was his last record as an engineer before going on to produce Guns N' Roses. Also, on the records we did with Nevison, besides being a great producer and having a clear idea of what he wanted to get done with the record, Ron himself was also a great engineer. He'd engineered for Led Zeppelin and Traffic and The Who, so he was an amazing engineer and producer. So the two of those guys together just made everything move more quickly." Detailing the band's recording schedule, Nevison recalled, "We came down to the Record Plant, when it was still on 3rd Street in L.A., and recorded the backing tracks. The album was recorded within probably a 10-day period, as far as the basic tracks went. We always recorded more tracks than we'd end up using, so there was usually 14 tracks, and we'd usually record one a day, sometimes two songs a day."

The efficiency with which the group laid their basic tracks allowed them a more relaxed pace when attention turned to overdubbing, at the Sausalito Record Plant in Northern California. As Heart producers before him had also found, recording the Wilson sisters' vocal tracks was an easy job for Nevison. "It's so easy to work with great singers," he attested, "and [Ann's] such an amazing singer, and I love her voice so much. She was so easy to record and Ann is still one of my favorite singers. Ann always came in very prepared, and she has great pitch. With Ann, she knew what to do; she is one of the most incredible singers in the entire world. I usually had to just push the record button. I remember how in awe I was of just having her in the studio; I was amazed. Nancy too was very, very good and very professional, so it was easy to record both of them. I loved their professionalism in the studio. Ann and Nancy had this great history of singing together since they were like five years old; they had a vocal blend that made me look good." Nancy, for her part, quipped that Ann had such vocal mastery in the studio that "truly any producer is lucky to record her voice; she needs no corrections." Nevison considered the Wilson sisters' vocal performances so precious that he even "recorded Ann and Nancy's warm-ups, because they think they're warming up, but it could be the best thing they've done all week. They don't think the red light's on yet, and sometimes they'd do things that were totally unexpected. The voice is fresh, so I always recorded the first thing." Still, in spite of his reverence for both sisters' considerable vocal gifts, Nevison treated them no differently from any of the other countless platinum artists he'd produced in years prior, stating that when he was producing Ann, "she would stand in front of a microphone and sing like anyone else."

Nevison recalled, "I would do vocal comps with them, because by the time I was recording Heart, I was using a Mitsibushi 32-track digital machine, which allowed me to do many vocal takes and then create a composite track, which was a best-of from the six or seven vocal tracks. And I did that with both sisters. With Ann, we would do an average of six to eight, sometimes ten, and I'd let them sing for a couple of hours, make notes, and you know, the more ore you go through, the more gold you find. And keeping to that routine of singing multiple takes in one session is much better than stopping and starting, dropping in, and going over and over one line. My method gave us a lot of freedom. I would occasionally make notes, have Ann sing a half-dozen times all the way through, and sometimes — even a great singer like Ann — will encounter a problem area with one little area of the song. And it's no good if you go through six or eight times, and still have that one area. So when the broader track was finished, if I had any little problem areas, I would have her go over those little areas until I got them right. Whatever that was: a lot of times, if you're doing a rock song, and it's a four-minute song, by the time you get to the last chorus, you're pretty tired. So sometimes I would have them take a break, then go and do the last chorus or end of the song, because it would be a lot fresher. So sometimes we did them in segments, rather than all the way through, if it was just too taxing on her vocal chords. But it was the same process of repetitive takes of that part, rather than the whole song."

Throughout this sometimes lengthy and involved process, Ann and Nancy Wilson were as dedicated as Levison himself was to perfection in the process, pointing to the fact that throughout recording, "Ann and Nancy were present for all of each other's vocal sessions, and collectively for pretty much everything else." Alongside Ann and Nancy Wilson throughout the entire vocal recording, Sue Ennis explained their constant presence was designed, in part, to counter-balance Nevison's all-business mood in the studio. "We always tried to keep a light mood in the studio during tracking, particularly working with Keith Olsen and then with Ron Nevison. I think Nance was the mediating voice when Ann was doing her vocals, and I was there too, and it was our job to soften whatever the producer was saying. So if one of those guys would say to Ann, 'Go again,' then Nance and I would hop on and say, 'It was really cool, but you didn't quite get the last note,' or 'That fill was kinda busy.' We'd give her a little more direction, because most producers, if they were just moving along, would say, 'Let's go, let's go,' and sometimes Ann just needed a little bit more support and encouragement. The producers put up with us being there, giving feedback. Any sensitive producer understood that the dynamic was one where they were going to get more out of Ann — and Nance too — if a sister's voice was there in her head through the phones. The mood was

Flower Children:
Sisters Ann, Nancy and
Lynn Wilson growing up in
the 1960s

Arriving at the Seattle airport, Heart is welcomed home from tour in 1980

Sue Ennis (top) and Ann
Wilson, lifelong friends,
share a love for songwriting
and for canine companions

Nancy Wilson plays her heart out for fans

Ann Wilson displays her multi-talented musical side in performances

Heart rocking out in 2006

crucial — and still is — for both Ann and Nance. In that atmosphere, I would say they're incapable of being open emotionally and available for the moment if it's not a fun, light, nurturing environment. That's chicks for ya."

> 'The mood was crucial — and still is — for both Ann and Nance.'

The recording of the album's overdubs began "once the bass and drums were cut for the *Heart* LP, which we did in L.A.," Nevison recalled, "and it was just Howard and the girls from then on for overdubs. And when we did the first Heart album, we agreed to do all the overdubs in Sausalito, which was equidistant between L.A. and Seattle. I always like to — if I can do it — have artists recording on the road, rather than in their hometown, because I have much more of a captive audience. They're less likely to be out with their friends at night after session, all those types of distractions, and are more likely to get down to hard work so they can go home." When it came time for the album's keyboard parts to be overdubbed, Ron Nevison called on old friend and collaborator Peter Wolf, lead singer for the J. Geils Band, to play on the hit single "Never," which "was written pretty much by Holly Knight, and the girls I believe contributed to the lyrics. Holly had brought two songs to that project, and we did both of them, 'All Eyes' and 'Never.' They both had a totally different look; Holly was a more modern songwriter, and I thought the album, because of Holly's songs, was much more well-balanced. Howard and I put the keyboard parts together on that song. Then I brought in Peter Wolf, from J. Geils Band, who was also an interesting attribute to that song, and to the record more broadly speaking. He came in and did overdubs, and was just a special, special keyboard player. He was cutting edge with sounds with synthesizers. He was a classically trained musician and great writer and had all the latest gear and was fantastic. He

> **'"Every second of the night; every moment I'm awake"**
> **— it cracked there.'**

was a great factor in contributing to that project as a player, who did the strings, all the synth stuff, because Heart didn't really have that kind of expertise in the band. So his contributions to that record, and song specifically, are notable. There was something unique to doing those ballads with him."

The album's layered keyboard sound, Nevison explained, was dictated in part by the fact that "the mid-'80s were the keyboard times — the times of digital synthesizers and multiple programs in pop rock. Now of course there were synthesizers even when I made *Quadraphenia* with Pete Townsend and The Who, but back then you had to plug in and tune because you couldn't keep any sounds. You'd do a sound, record it, then you'd have to unplug everything and re-tune. But with the age of the DX-7 and some of the more modern synths in the early '80s, where you could store all these sounds, it was amazing. Because up till then, doing rock 'n' roll, you had very few options. You had acoustic and electric guitars, you had a fender Rhodes keyboard or Wurlitzer, acoustic piano or Hammond organ. And that was it. Of course you could have horns and strings and orchestrations, but they were all separate instruments to record. Then all of a sudden in the '80s: *boom*. You have strings, 20 different electric pianos, poly synths, all of these wonderful things. And that aided us greatly on the Heart albums where keyboards were appropriate and made sense."

When attention turned from "Never" to another of the album's hit keyboard-driven ballads, "These Dreams," a serendipitous moment during the song's recording became one of its vocal signatures. Nevison described this happy accident, "When we cut the track, Nancy had a cold, and so she kind of had this emotion, like a cracking in her voice. 'Every second of the night; every moment I'm awake' — it cracked there. So when I went to do the vocal, I did a bunch of tracks, and really loved the emotion she had in her voice during those parts. So I comped in a few words that cracked a little bit into the main final take." Leese recalled that circumstantially "it was a little different with 'These Dreams' because Nancy had always had an album track, pretty much on each record. There were a number of tunes Nancy sang, but never something that was going to be a single until the *Heart* record. We'd been looking for a song for Nancy to sing on that record, and 'These Dreams' had been bouncing around, and Nevison thought it was a great song. Bernie Taupin had written it, and we thought it would be perfect for Nancy because the song suited her voice and persona. So we recorded it and cut the basic track, and Nancy was really sick that day, so when it got to the part in the chorus vocal of 'Every moment I'm awake,' the higher notes in the song, her voice cracked because she was ill. So Ron was cutting the track just as a reference vocal, then a couple months later we went back in to do the real vocal, and Nancy comes in and is all healthy and fine, and she sings and hits those notes perfectly. Then we listened to it, and I don't remember who it was, but someone, I think Ron, said, 'I miss the cracking parts from the guide vocal. There's a certain vulnerability and empathy that the listener gets when you hear her straining to hit these notes. You're subconsciously rooting for her in a way.' So we went back in and got the bad notes from the original guide vocal, took the flaws and imported them onto the perfect vocal."

According to Nevison, that magic moment almost didn't make it into the final edit. "What happened was Christmas break was coming up, so I recorded the lead vocal, comped that in and we made tapes and everyone went on holiday. So when we all got back to the studio after break in January of 1985, Nancy told me, 'My mom says my voice is cracking.' And I said, '*No!* Please,

please don't change anything, it's perfect!' And they agreed to go with it. It's in the chorus, and it's very important." Another wise vocal decision on Nevison's part during tracking was to bring in a list of star-studded back-up vocalists, on "These Dreams": "Johnny Cola from Huey Lewis and Grace Slick for backgrounds on that ballad." Nancy and that song seemed destined for one another from the start, Sue Ennis remembered. "The night that Ron and Peter Wolf played that song for Ann and Nancy, there were a bunch of songs on that tape, but when that song came on, Nancy *jumped* off the couch and ran and threw her arms around the speaker, and said, 'I claim this. I don't care if I don't do anything else on this album, this is my song. I want this song, I want to sing this song, I want this song. . . .' So everybody — including Ann — started laughing and went, 'Okay, okay, yes!' Ann was like, 'God Con, I've never seen you so adamant about anything.' And Nancy said, 'I know! It's *mine*.' It maybe had to do with the fact that it was written by Bernie Taupin, who was a great hero of ours. So she just made a claim, and it was like, 'Great, this was meant to be.' And Nancy sang the hell out of it in the studio, and Ann was there cheering her along. When it became the first #1 single for Heart, there wasn't any weird feeling between them. Ann took it well, this crazy twist that after all these years, it was Nance who sang the big song. She was also *thrilled* that her band finally had a #1 single."

Attention turned from vocals to rhythm and lead guitar tracking; Nevison was set to bring the rock back to Heart. "When the group shook up its line-up in the early '80s, Nancy went from playing acoustic guitar to electric rhythm guitar, and Howard went from rhythm guitar to lead guitar, so they both stepped into positions that had been previously held by other players. And Howard was not writing the kind of riffy things that Roger Fisher had, and as good as a musician as Howard is, he's very much a journeyman. He could play anything, but he wasn't the same guitar player as Roger had been, certainly in terms of

writing. He didn't come up with the riffs, and I think that's what led to their demise with Epic. They were great at doing *Dog and Butterfly*, but after Roger left, [they] didn't have that rock edge that everybody expected them to have. So when I signed on board, I made sure the band rocked out again."

Lead guitarist Leese undoubtedly played a large role in that, describing a set-up "on the *Heart* album, where the change was huge because in 1980 I had a guitar built for me by Paul Reed Smith called 'The Golden Eagle,' which was the first PRS guitar with a maple top, made from a 300-year-old piece of furniture. I paid $2,000 for it, and today it's worth $500,000. It was an epic-sounding guitar, a really amazing instrument. So I'd brought in 20 guitars, and me and Ron went through all of them, and this one by far sounded the best. It had a really big, powerful sound, and we found that when we would want to get Ann to do the vocal, if I hadn't put on that big, heavy guitar, she wouldn't sing that big and loud. I would have to put the heavy guitar on first so that would inspire her to really scream and sing big. In addition, we found a Marshall stack, and he insisted on using that for everything. I'd suggest we try something else, and he'd always say, 'No, no, no, get the Golden Eagle.' That was the guitar I played on both the records we made with Ron, and is the guitar sound of those records. As far as micing, I would run two 4 by 12 cabinets, and we would mic them both — one close-miced and one a little bit off into the room a little bit. As far as mics, we used 57s, or sometimes a 57 and a 414, or sometimes even a Neumann vocal mic, but the close mics were always 57s. There were very few effects. Once we had the guitar sound done, Ron wouldn't change it. He wouldn't do anything to it, he was funny that way. He also realized that, a lot of times, my first take would be my best, so he'd come in, we'd be getting all the levels and sounds, and he'd go, 'Okay, run it down for me one more time,' and I'd play it one more time, and he'd go, 'Okay, you're done.' And I'd go, 'Wait, we haven't even done take one.' And he'd go, 'Yep, that was take one,

Management:
FRONT LINE/
TRUDY GREEN
(213) 859-1900

L:R   Mark Andes, Ann Wilson, Howard Leese, Nancy Wilson, Denny Carmassi

HEART

I just didn't tell you.' And I'd go, 'Come on, let me have some fun, let me play it for a while.' And he'd go, 'Tell you what, I'm gonna go eat lunch and give you a half hour. If you have anything better than that, we'll use it.' I remember specifically the song 'Bad Animals,' the solo on that, on take one, he goes, 'You're not going to do better, I know you. That's the take.' And I said, 'Well, I'm gonna try,' so I sit there while he and Mike Clink work for a half hour, and he came back and sure enough, the first one was the best. I didn't think we were recording, and wasn't worried about it, and was just playing off the top of my head."

With a nod to the rhythm section Howard Leese had assembled, Nevison recalled, "Denny Carmassi was just an amazing drummer. We had a really great rhythm section, and they had a great attitude, so tracking was just a really easy thing to do with these guys. This was a great group. I've had groups — without saying any names — where the rhythm sections presented some very tacky areas I had to polish up — but Heart was not. This was a great team, it was fresh, and they were all consummate musicians." The technical mic set-up he used to record Carmassi followed Nevison's set of norms for drum tracks: "First of all, find the right room to record drums in, which was Studio D at the Record Plant. It was a pretty big, good sounding drum room. I usually used a D-20 mic for the kick drum, an SM-57 for the snare. For overheads, I usually tried to use good, warm tube mics, like U67s. I would put a KM-84 on the high-hat, and for room mics, sometimes I would rent mics, depending what they had on-hand, but always tried to use U87s or FAT mics. And I recorded them straight into the board. Bass and rhythm guitar were also recorded live off the floor, but I very rarely used anything but the drums. When I cut drum tracks, I would have everybody in there, but would redo everything and just keep the bed drum track. Because you can devote all your time and energy to getting just one track sounding good when you're cutting a bunch of tracks, with five different musicians. It's tough to kind of devote enough time for that, so that's why I always started out focusing on drums."

As an engineer *and* producer, Ron Nevison had the unique ability — unlike many record producers who know nothing about the technical side of mixing — to wear both hats at the same time. "I used to like to get one mix a day, and of course, with Heart, I had the budget to do this, but I would work all day on a mix, then get it to the point where I thought it was almost there. Then I would leave it up overnight — that was the only way to get space from it. I would then drive home, listen to it, listen to it at home, get up in the morning and listen to it, and very often, within ten minutes of getting back behind the console, it was finished, because I knew exactly what to do. So for the girls, there was no reason for them to come in at noon, they would come in at six or seven and listen to the last two hours and make suggestions then. So with Heart, I would give them cassette tapes at the mix session at day's end, and they'd listen in their cars, houses, etcetera, the same as I did, then we would come in the morning, and they would give me their suggestions, comments. I'd incorporate them at our first listening session, and then they'd leave. Then I'd start on the next song, work all day on my own getting the mix, then they'd come back at five or six o'clock, make a first round of suggestions on the new song and then I'd incorporate those in, make tapes for everyone to listen to, and the next morning, if we were all satisfied, we'd move onto the next song. If changes were needed, we'd make them. So that's how it went on."

To no surprise, both Wilson sisters were very involved in the approval part of the mixing process, with the producer explaining that "Ann and Nancy liked to sit in during the mixing of album vocals; they were around. But Nancy was certainly much more into the whole recording process than Ann was, I think possibly also because Nancy was the guitar player, which added dynamically to what she was contributing and had opinions on. Howard was around also a lot." Howard's role was advocate for the band for some of the more monotonous decisions during mixing. "I was the guy who went to every Heart mixing session. I was the one representing the band. I knew the band most intimately in terms of how we wanted to sound, and would work with the producers toward that end, to get something I thought the band would be happy with as well. At the end of the day, we'd make tapes, and have a version with Ann's voice at this level, and Ann's voice up a decibel and up two decibels, and take them home, listen, make our comments and come in the next day and make adjustments." From Nancy's perspective, "mixing an album is very delicate. To start over and zero everything out from scratch with a mix often brings nothing better to the table than you already had, and magic can slip away so

> '. . . often unplanned little mistakes or rough edges are better left in.'

easily. Every little setting can mean a huge shift in the character of the song if it's tampered with by the usual over thinking or 'over gigging.' But I think the biggest mix decision is the relationship of the vocal level to the track. If the vocal is too up front, the track loses its claws, and vice versa. That's the value of good compressors and mics. Another thing I've come to learn about mixing is how to leave in the human elements. There are often unplanned little mistakes or rough edges that are better left in."

The final mixing decisions ended up having a big impact on the success of the album's singles. Nevison recalled, "['Never'] had a great hooky intro, but the guitar was also doing the same thing. I remember for a single, we had a hit single with 'What About Love,' and 'Never' was picked as the next single, and I remember going in to remix it, and Holly Knight came along. She had told Grierson that she thought the mix I had done on the album was too safe, so I listened to it and agreed. So we went in, and it was a good collaborative effort: Ann and Nancy were there and Holly was there and we remixed it at the Record Plant. I didn't use as many of the guitars, and there are some holes in the verses. I left 'Hey baby I'm talking to you,' and just had the keyboard shine through instead of having the guitars up all the way. All in all, it was a much better, more dynamic mix." Turning to a far more complicated and equally as significant single, "These Dreams," Nevison began by explaining that, as with "Never," "I edited the song after it was cut, and I don't think the sisters even heard it as a single until I cut out to the second verse.

The original version brought the chorus in fairly quickly, and then all of a sudden, they went, 'Wow, that's a single.' See, I had to shorten it for it to be a single. It went intro, verse, intro, verse, before it got to the chorus, and the verses were fairly long. So I shortened it to intro, verse, chorus, and the same thing repeated. In fact, I don't even think the song was considered by the label for a single until I made the edits."

Amazingly, even after Nevison's additional editing, Heart's label was initially resistant to releasing the song as a single, while the band had an instinctive feeling about it. Leese explained, "We had a song we thought was a hit, and told the label we wanted it to be the third single. And they said, 'You're crazy, no, no, no. We have all this momentum. We just had two top 10 singles. The album's starting to really move. You guys are going to kill this album dead in its tracks.' Our manager also thought it was suicide because of Nancy, because everyone knew Ann's voice, so they were like, 'It's a total left turn; you can't do it. We're not gonna let you do it.' So we told them, 'Read our contract. We have total creative control over everything — you can't tell us what to do.' And our thinking was 'Imagine what it would be like if we had two star singles, with two girls in the band both with hit songs.' And our final retort to everyone was 'Well, it's our career and our money, so that's the way we want to do it,' and it turned out to be our first number one single of that era. Our manager was a big enough gentleman after that to call us and go, 'Okay, from now on, we'll do the opposite of whatever I say, and everything will be fine.' He admitted, 'You guys were right, everyone else was wrong,' and for us, that was a really sweet day."

The song's success was also an extraordinarily personal victory for Nevison, as he'd been the first to nurture it along as a single for Nancy. The producer recalled feeling a sense of validation given the fight he and the band had put up on its behalf. "The thing about 'These Dreams,' the fact is that it was the third hit single, and there were other things before it that I had heard as singles. I had maybe envisioned it as a single, but never a number one single. But the way the whole album was set up, with 'What About Love' being a really strong single, and then 'Never' really kicking ass, it set up Nancy's voice with a ballad for the third single. It was perfect. It worked out just like I planned it. I'll never forget that I was in Hawaii with my managers on holiday, and we used to call in the morning to find out how many adds at radio we'd gotten, on a Tuesday or Wednesday, and I remember calling from a phone booth, and found out that we had 147 CHR ads, and there were only 174 stations. And when I got off the phone, my face was white. So we had radio's ear after that."

Addressing how Ann handled the song's success given that it was the band's first hit without her singing lead vocal, Nevison offered, "in terms of Nancy's singing what became the biggest hit on the album, on the other side, there's the jealousy I'm sure between the two sisters, but I know Nancy was really happy she had a number one single." Leese added, "I think on Ann's part, there was a little bit of warming up needed there to the idea of Nancy singing a lead, because when they went number one, that was a whole different dynamic because now Nancy had sung on the biggest Heart song ever. That album was a huge success, we had two top 10 singles out on the same day with 'These Dreams' and 'Nothing at All.' It was a pretty amazing time." Nancy explained to a journalist that she considered her and her sister Ann to be above such insignificant squabbles. "I think a lot of the reason for that is that Ann and I are sisters. She's someone who has known me before I was even born. The music has always kept us friends because there is more to worry about than petty rivalries. If we were just one girl out in a world of boys, without a really good friend to talk to and to lean on, it would just be a little bit too tough."

Heart's gambles — in trusting Nevison's outside song choices, and once they had made those songs their own, in fighting for their promotion at radio — paid off handsomely upon the album's release in June 1985. Though it was the band's ninth studio LP, it was their first to hit #1 on the Billboard Top 200 Album chart in more than five years. *Heart* sold more than 10 million copies, driven by four Top 10 smash singles, "What About Love," "Never," "Nothing At All" and the album's biggest-selling single, "These Dreams." *Rolling Stone* hailed the group's comeback LP as "enticing and brooding. . . . [It's] exciting because it offers evidence that the band still has talent and smarts . . . such ventures are where Heart's future . . . lies." Heart's self-titled Capitol Records debut would spend 92 weeks on the charts. Following a massively successful world arena tour, the band wasted no time re-entering the studio in late 1986 to begin work on their follow-up, *Bad Animals*.

Preparing to record *Bad Animals*, the resistance to songs not penned by the band was still strong, despite the commercial success of Heart's singles. Nevison recalled, "They were never happy about having to record other people's songs. They weren't happy about it this time [with *Bad Animals*] either. And I had gotten a song from Tom Kelly and Billy Steinberg called 'Alone,' which I thought would be perfect for them. 'Who Will You Run To' was another we got from Diane Warren. So, again, while Ann and Nancy would have preferred to do their own songs, I think they realized they needed singles. They had written lots of hits, but it's just they weren't writing material suitable for that time in terms of what radio would rotate. We're talking about 1986, so their singles had to be suitable for the airwaves for contemporary hit radio. The way to sell millions of records at that time was to have your rockers on AOR rock radio, and your singles on CHR radio, which was the pop aspect of it. If you just rocked out, you'd sell 200,000 records, but you could sell 2,000,000 copies if you were on CHR radio. So what I'm saying is they were open to doing singles, but would have preferred doing their own material. That wasn't exclusive to Heart either, I used to have to drag

HEART

BAD ANIMALS

groups kicking and screaming onto the pop charts in those days. They enjoyed the success we had with that formula on *Heart*, so with *Bad Animals*, our formula was similar to the first album. They also knew what was expected from them by Don Grierson at Capitol Records, and they went along with it."

Howard Leese conceded, "There were times where people in the band were pissed off about it, ironically, for instance, with 'Alone.' I remember when we got the demo, and we're rehearsing at Nancy's house, and she walked out of rehearsal and her own house she hated the song so much. So I said, 'The demo is very, very pop. Let us play it our way as a band. Let us record the demo, and then decide, because it won't sound like the demo, it will sound like a Heart song.' So when we recorded it, we did the demo while Nancy pouted upstairs, and then she came around to seeing that it was a powerful song. Those guys were great writers, and I thought it was a great song, but in that process there were a few toes stepped on and feelings were hurt here and there. But that's what being in a band's all about — you're not a solo artist, and there's give and take. Everyone's working toward the same thing, all on the same team, wanting it to be as great as it could be."

Nevison used much of the same technical set-up he had in the course of recording their first collaboration together. "I remember staying up in Seattle, rehearsing up there again. We recorded in L.A., and did the drum tracks at A&M, and then we cut the rest of the backing tracks at One on One Studio. We did the overdubs at Can Am in the San Fernando Valley. Ann and Nancy were there for the whole process, and again, because we were recording away from home, even though it was L.A., they were there to do the album. We also did some of the vocals in New York because Ann and Nancy wanted to go Christmas shopping, so we did two weeks at the Hit Factory in New York. And while we were recording, everyone was welcome to voice their opinions. I did have a problem with the bass player Mark Andes, and I really liked Mark. He was a really good bass player, and worked really well with Denny Carmassi. Anyway, usually we'd cut the tracks and the drummer's finished, and so on with the bass, and then you're left with overdubs. So Mark had ideas about stuff we tried when he was tracking. So when he was finished up, he took off, and for the next five weeks we were overdubbing, and then at the end of that five weeks Mark showed up again and said, 'What happened to this, what happened to that?' And I said, 'You can't come after five weeks of not being here. Every day, I make decisions, every hour, on things, and you weren't here when we tried things that didn't work.' And when I say we, I mean me and the band, they had been there with me, and Mark hadn't. So we had a fight and he walked out, and I never saw him again. That's unfortunate that that happened, and we were both probably to blame, but the lesson was you have to be there if you want to have an opinion. But all in all, that was the only moment in the album where there was any friction."

As for the rest of the band, Leese recalled, "We were just on a roll — everybody knew what they were doing, we had a great producer, and had all the best songwriters working for us, so you could feel that we were in high gear. Ron as a producer was demanding, and at times a little hard to work for because if you weren't at the top of your game, he'd send you home and do something else. He wanted the best out of everybody all the time, which is the way it's gotta be. He extended that to Ann and Nancy as well, as you'll notice with the songwriting. They had songs, and he would sometimes say, 'No, we're not using this one; I want to use this one.' He wanted to make sure ahead of time that he'd have the authority to do that and that they would listen, and to his credit, he was right." Given the massive comeback the band had mounted off the success of their last album, Leese admitted he "felt the pressure, but not an intimidating kind of pressure, but a little bit empowering because I knew I needed to bring my A game. For instance, heading into the recording of *Bad Animals*, we knew that 'Alone' would be the

> 'This song is going to be number one, so the solo better be pretty good.'

first single, and that it would be a hit song while we were recording it. I remember being in my hotel room the night before I had to do the solo, thinking, 'This song is going to be number one, so the solo better be pretty good.' The other thing I wanted to do as a soloist is take the energy from the lead vocal that she hands over to me when the solo starts and I have to start at the level she's at, and if possible raise it up a little bit, bring the intensity up, and when I hand it back to the lead vocal, she's now higher still. It's your job as the soloist to take over for the lead vocal and bring it up a notch. That was the one case where I knew that song was going to be number one, I could just tell. 'Who Will You Run To,' another single off that album, was a Diane Warren song. We learned that in two days, and that was the finished track you heard on the radio. Ron engineered that album himself, and there were just beautiful recordings when we were done."

By that point, Ann and Nancy Wilson seemed to have come to terms with the role their looks played in the marketing of their music, given MTV's status as the primary promotional vehicle of the time. Heart had the the sisters' striking beauty to capitalize on, which Nevison pointed out as an advantage, reasoning that "it worked both ways, because when MTV came around, and Christopher Cross had had this big album out, and did one of the network's first videos. Well, after he appeared on MTV, no one wanted to go sailing with him anymore." The new power the group had in shaping their image was one that Nancy Wilson felt conflicted about, as she revealed to a journalist years later. "Sex can be used to our advantage and it can be used for the wrong reasons. I think a lot of women get really annoyed that Madonna goes as far as she does sometimes. But then again, you've got to hand it to her for being that gutsy. I guess I'm on the fence. There's some things I don't like about blatant sexuality, but as long as someone can back it up with real talent, then there's no gripe. But when you get someone like Vanity, where it's pretty see through, it's a little bit thin, there's not a lot of substance. . . . Image-wise [it] . . . was a conscious decision to come out with the bold colors. We wanted to have a look that was really hard and really soft at the same time. That's how our music is. Like the really striking blatant colors are the primary opposites of everything. The colors are loud and hard and then there's a soft edge to it. There's a frill here and a little lace there. So, it's got the feminine touch, like our music."

Rolling Stone paid Heart a compliment in terms of how successfully they had adapted to the demands of the times without losing their artistic credibility, concluding in their review of *Bad Animals* that "the Wilson sisters and their bandmates know how to make the formula yield valid, vital hard pop. . . . *Bad Animals* is savvy and spirited; it could give stadium rock a good name. Or a better one, at least." Released in June 1987, *Bad Animals* debuted at #2 on Billboard's Top 200 Album Chart, quickly going double-platinum off the strength of the #1 smash single "Alone," as well as two other Top 20 hits, "Who Will You Run To" and "There's the Girl." By that point in the band's 12-year career, Heart's live audiences included as many teenagers as it did their parents; by successfully reinventing their sound they introduced their music to an entirely new generation of fans. That audience would grow even larger with the release of the band's tenth studio LP, *Brigade*, as the 1980s came to a close.

HEARt

BRIGADE

CHAPTER 10

Brigade

1989–1991

Emerging out of the 1980s as one of the biggest living legends in pop rock, Heart was at the top of its game. A key force in re-launching Ann and Nancy Wilson almost five years earlier, producer Ron Nevison recalled the events leading up to what would have been his third LP with Heart, "I was doing an album with Patty Smyth, and there was a song that I wanted Heart to do on the *Bad Animals* LP, but they didn't want to do it, and it was another Billy Steinberg/Tom Kelly song, and so when I got to do Patty's album, I had her do it. Well, at some point, Nancy called up and said, 'I want to do that song for a film I'm doing with my husband.' And I said, 'Well I'm doing it with Patty.' And she said, 'What? You're doing it with Patty?' And I said, 'You didn't want to do it.' So they went and got Ritchie Zito to do a song for the film, and said, 'We like Ritchie now.' And that was it. I remember having a meeting with them in a hotel room in L.A. about the third album, and thought everything was set, and then out of the blue heard they wanted to work with Ritchie. After selling 10 million albums with me. So I have to tell you that I had a great time on both the albums I did with them, in spite of the fact that I did not end on a great note. I was disappointed in that, but I am still very proud of those albums. For me, the greatest parts of those two albums will always be the day I found those songs, 'Alone' and 'These Dreams,' and they turned out to be #1 hits. And I'm proud of the fact we took it from where we started to there. I'm not happy that after two albums with such success that I was turned away like that. But I understand that's the business, and still consider my work with them to be one of my career highlights. I had a ball. And I hope they did too!"

From the band's perspective, guitarist Howard Leese explained, "Ritchie Zito was our first choice for producer on that album, I don't remember anyone else being spoken about. After we'd done *Bad Animals*, Nevison was off on something else, so he wasn't available. It wasn't like it was a matter of 'Let's not use him again,' because we were doing better than we'd ever been as a result of that collaboration, selling crazy amounts of records and playing gigantic shows. Everybody was thrilled at how successfully we were doing, being as big as a band could be and loving it. By the time we worked with Ritchie, they were happy to have somebody new, and we felt a kinship for him musically because he was a guitar player and played in Elton John's band, spoke the language and was a real nice guy. As a producer, he had a really good pop sensibility, and had done some great rock-pop records, and I just thought it was a good fit for the band. He spoke our language, and again, wanted to bring in great material, so we learned a lot of songs for that record and picked the best ones irrespective of who wrote it. If the girls had a great song, it made the record. And if there were ten other songs that

Howard Leese   Ann Wilson   Mark Andes   Nancy Wilson   Danny Carmassi

HEART

were better, then they wouldn't make the record. So in a way that fostered competition and everybody having to raise the bar on their own writing because now we're competing with the best writers in the business. *Brigade* is definitely my favorite Heart album from the '80s stuff, and Zito was my favorite producer because he was a nice guy to be around ten hours a day, seven days a week in the studio." Longtime Wilson sisters' confidant Sue Ennis noted, "Ritchie Zito was much more emotionally available, maybe, than Ron Nevison had been. He was just a softer, nicer, easy-going guy, and I think that made the recording experience easier for Ann and Nance. I know they felt supported by him in the studio."

Ritchie Zito, for his part, recalled the shift from one producer to the next, "Because Nevison and the band had done really well on the prior two albums, they weren't in trouble when they came to me. Heart was looking to make a change. It becomes adversarial at times trying to get an artist to record songs they didn't really want to record, and that really cost their last producer his relationship with them, because when you fight that hard toe-to-toe with an artist, it created tension, and at a certain point, they didn't want to make records anymore together. I still had to do the same thing, except perhaps with a different bedside manner. Ron might have been a tougher guy, and I might have had a softer sell. Still, I worked hard on that record."

Zito saw his role as producer as "sort of your tour guide through the recording process. I've always made records the same way: you try to set the stage, try to get the artist in the right place. People don't realize a lot of the work is picking the right song, the right arrangement, the right key, the right tempo, and you've done half the job already. Making sure the lyric is right, because it's like a script, they have to have something interesting to sing. It's got to be cleverly written, and have words that sound great with notes. If that's not there, it's going to be hard to get a good vocal. So a lot of that work is done in advance, whether you're cognizant of it or not. It's like a football game: most of the choices you make before you get on the field decide the outcome. So the more I know what it's gonna be like in advance, the more I can dictate the outcome. I don't like wild cards, or super

surprises. The stronger the song upon entry into the process of recording, the better the outcome."

Once pre-production had wrapped, Zito recalled, "Most of the bed tracks were cut with Denny, Mark and Howard, then when the basic tracks were done and everything was cool, Howard and I would spend a day in the studio doing lead guitar and keyboards, and Nancy would add her acoustic tracks." For Leese, working with Zito was a special thrill because "a guitar player produced [the album], and he let me play. There's guitar all over that record; he let me take the time to do what I wanted to do, was open to all of my ideas. Each song had a big showcase place for the solo, and it was just a real guitarsy record. I used the Golden Eagle again, same Marshall stack. He had a great engineer, Phil Kafel, working with him as well." The respect between guitarist and producer was mutual. Zito explained, "A lot of what keeps a band a band is sort of their sociological functionality, and the politics within the structure of a four- or five-member community, and Howard Leese was a very diplomatic personality, very easy to get along with and very musical. He'd sit there, and the two of us would orchestrate the track — we'd start with basic guitar, drums and bass, and between the two of us with my input and his performance and ideas, he was able to orchestrate the guitars and keyboards we did."

In capturing the album's drum sound, Ritchie Zito explained, "Records that were made in the '80s, everything was so gigantic, larger than life, very cartoon-like. So we worked very hard, all the time, on our drum sound. I would only work at a studio called One on One, or what used to be A&M studios, premiere studios. I really, really liked big fucking rooms, so that I could have the benefit of large, ambient snare drums and tom toms when appropriate. We had this PA we would rent, and we'd stick kick drums and sometimes tom toms into the PA and re-amplify into the room, then mic the room with the kick and the tom toms being amplified through the giant PA. So we went to great extents to try and make the drum sounds bigger and beefier. Back then, the drum sound was a big, defining aspect of production. In terms of mics, we used 57s a lot over the tom toms and the snares, and 414s on the overheads. Also, at the time, AMS was a new company, and they came out with non-linear reverbs, which were all over the snare." As for the keyboards on *Brigade*, "Luckily back then it was almost all analog synths. We used the Jupiter 8 a lot, and then with the advent of the Yamaha DX7, which was the first digital synth, we used that. But I liked the way the Jupiter 8 sounded and was pretty familiar with it. I knew my way around it. I also liked the Juno 60, which was like half of a Jupiter 8. The Mini-moog was great for synth stuff. But we did use the DX7 on that album for the Fender Rhodes sound."

As for recording the album's stellar vocal tracks, Zito felt he had a huge advantage, "Ann's voice is just second to none, frankly. There are very few females in rock 'n' roll; it's not hard to count all the girls that have been forces in rock history in the past 50 years. There haven't been that many, it's been a pretty male-dominated world in the rock business, and I can't think of anyone like Ann. Ann had that voice that you could hear in the back of the arena, and Nancy had a completeness too. She was a really good acoustic guitar player, she had her own musical per-sonality that Ron Nevison started to bring out in 'These Dreams.' I think Ann especially liked that, but I didn't get her to do too much raspyness when I was working with her, I tried to bring out some of the more natural sound in her voice. But the two of them together were Heart, and it was a magical combina-tion. They each brought something to the relationship. Each of them certainly could have fronted bands that would have been successful for many kinds of sounds. Ann definitely had a stronger, more powerful voice, but Nancy was a great singer and great musician. Both are very, very uniquely talented ladies. When recording vocals, they both were very good, they were pros."

As she had with every previous album, Zito recalled, "Nancy

was [at the studio] a lot. They came together, and had rented a house not far from where I was living. So they came together to the studio most of the time, because Nancy would

sing a lot of harmonies, and they would certainly suggest things to each other. They were definitely there in the studio for one another's vocal performances. I remember when we were doing vocals, in the control room, there was this little alcove right behind the console, and there was this little couch where one or the other would sit when the other was singing. So it wasn't like either of the sisters was sitting next to me pressing the talk-back button; it wasn't really like that. But when one came in, the other would have a few words together about the performance, but it was very relaxed. Things were made additionally easier because of Ann and Nancy's natural sibling tonality. Brothers and sisters genetically have similarities in the bone structure, and the size of the esophagus, the size of the chin, all that stuff where the tone reverberates in a similar size, and it all leads to vocals coming out sounding similar.

"I've always been attracted to artists with distinct voices. I've always been a big fan of voices, such that I always picked my projects for the most part that way: Ann Wilson, Robin Zander, Eddie Money, Joe Cocker, Kenny Loggins, John Waite and Cher. Whenever I had a chance to work with a distinctive voice, I was in; that's what suckered me every time. Where John Waite and Eddie Money played more to the storyteller, intimate voice, Ann Wilson could hit the back of the arena. So I was majorly drawn to that. Ann was unbelievable, and hard for me sometimes, because it was all so good. She walked up to the microphone, opened her mouth and it was like, 'Oh my God.' Every time, that's what it was. I wish it was harder, and that I could tell you stories, I can't. She was pretty special." Zito and the band soon established a routine for tracking, he recalled. "For that album, we did demos; that was our blueprint. Once the basic tracks were done, and it came to vocals, like most singers, we'd do late afternoon or early evening, between five and seven, recording sessions, and start the process. And Ann would just walk in, stand in front of the mic and just sing. And I'd say, 'Okay, let's do another take,' then we'd take a little break, for five minutes or maybe not, [have] a glass of water, and in 20 minutes, I had six performances, one better than the next; I didn't know what to do. We tracked that album at a studio called One on One, which was great because it had an SSL console, and had bought a Neve console and gutted it, so they had a stand-alone rack of 20 some-odd modules of Neve mic and EQs, so it was the best of all worlds back then.

"I used tube mics all the time on vocals. I also liked having the lyric in front of me when someone's singing, but I never write anything down, ever. I know most producers that I've seen work have chalkboards or white boards where they write down or check stuff off. But my approach is every day, I open up the tracks and listen to what's missing, as opposed to what I think is missing. I always looked at it like: put them in the right place, put them in the right mood, get it going, press the button and pray to God it comes out great. Then, when it wasn't going well, use what I always felt — because I had been a musician of some consequence in my first career playing with Elton John — that I had immediate credibility with the artist I was producing when I walked in the room. I was one of them, so I always had that respect of really knowing what a C-chord was, and being able to play a C-chord, and when I suggested we do an A-minor instead of a C, I didn't talk metaphorically in colors, I could talk in notes and chords. So when it came to vocals, I really prided myself on getting really great vocals out of artists, most I did all the same way: I would let them do full performances, and then I would pick my favorite stuff. Sometimes you don't get a line, then you have to make them sing it over and over, but that's not always the best way to get music. I like to let the person perform, and look at it as a whole piece, a whole song. With Ann Wilson from Heart, because female voices tend to be a bit higher, I used a U49 mic on her vocals for that album."

The LP's greatest challenge turned out to ultimately be its greatest hit as well: "All I Wanna Do (Is Make Love to You)." Leese recalled, "Mutt Lange makes demos that are so good they sound like Def Leppard records. You could put them out as singles they are so perfect. On that song, it was a great demo when we got it but we thought, 'This is a great song, but it's not going to work because it's got a guy singing.' And I said, 'What if we turn it around, have the girls sing it, and say she picked up the guy to use him to get pregnant?' So that's what made the whole thing work. The funny thing is we cut that track, and there was a little guitar part on the b-section of the second part of the verse, a little ding-ding-ding, broken note, real tiny little part. And when I cut it, I changed the order of two of the notes, and we're in the studio, and I get a phone call — which never happens — and they go, 'It's Mutt Lange calling for Howard from London.' And I go, 'Really?' because I'd never even spoken to the guy. So I pick up the phone and he goes, 'Howard, you changed the part. You're going ding-ding-ding, instead of ding-ding-ding, it's got to be this way.' And I go, 'Well, I didn't think it mattered. It's just a little part,' and I thought that this way was as good or maybe even better. I liked it a little bit better. . . . And he goes, 'No, no, no, you don't understand. It's got to be my way.' And I go, 'Well, I don't think it's that big of a deal, so I guess we'll just agree to disagree.' And again he goes, 'No, no, no, no, you've got to go in and re-record it.' And I said, 'I don't think I do. I think it's already done and fine.'

"He was really a control guy, and had the belief that I needed to do it his way because his demo was perfect. In the end, I kept it my way. In terms of the lyrics, I think he was happy it worked because someone was recording it. There was a whole

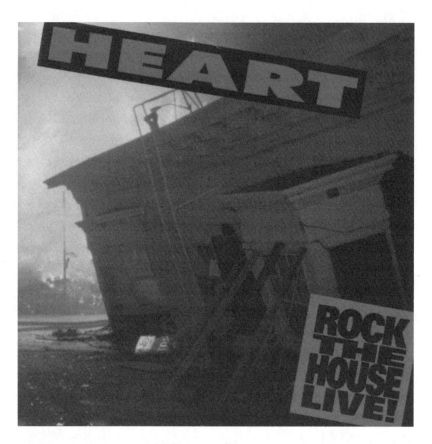

Heart's 1990 live album, **Rock the House Live!**

other half of a verse that we dropped because it didn't make sense with a girl singing it. I just did a little edit, and it was one of the few times I ever had anything to do with any of the lyrics, and because it wasn't the girls' lyrics, it was okay. I just had an idea that if we turned this around, chopped this half of the verse off, then the girl can sing it, and it's kind of more interesting because she's using the guy instead of the other way around, which is more typical. Then he sees the child and his own eyes, and goes, 'Oh man, I got her pregnant that night.' That's what made it work."

Elaborating on the song's development, Zito explained, "We got that song after Mutt Lange had first sent it over to Don

Henley, and it didn't make sense for him, and I was right at the tail end of the Bad English record, so it didn't make sense to introduce it to them. The Heart record was coming up and it made good sense to play it for Ann and Nancy. That song was written from a male perspective, so we had to do some slight adjustments to make it from a female perspective, not many, but slight adjustments lyrically — he to she, and she to he, and there was a surprise in the lyric about a pregnancy, so we had some adjustments to make. The chorus to that song was just so freakin' strong, when I heard it, I went, 'Jesus.' Mutt Lange wrote one of the best pop songs period, forget about it. That songwriting gift doesn't go to a lot of people, but it went to him."

Addressing the production of the album's other hit single, "Stranded," on which Nancy Wilson sang lead, Leese recalled, "Nancy sang on this song, and that song came late in the day, at first we couldn't find a song for her to do. Jamie Kyle wrote that song, and someone brought it in, and we thought, 'Ah, here it is. This is perfect for Nancy.'" Zito expanded, "I got it from a publisher, Wrensongs, and the song just caught my ear, and I thought Nancy sang it really, really well. I think I felt it was clear that Nancy should sing it, and Ann was very supportive." Recording Nancy, the producer would "get five or six takes, and pick the best parts." Leese also recalled that recording the song was "fun because the clean guitar on that song is Ritchie. He wanted to do a cameo, and we thought that was a perfect spot: a nice little clean guitar in the verse."

Ultimately, both "All I Wanna Do (Is Make Love to You)" and "Stranded" would become top 10 smashes, with the former debuting at #1 on the Billboard Top 40 Pop Singles Chart, driving the album to a #3 debut. *Rolling Stone* praised the album's "guts" and "charm."

CHAPTER 11

Desire Walks On

1992–1994

By the fall of 1992 with the success of *Brigade*, Heart was once again one of the biggest pop rock bands in the world. They had earned enough capital from the more than 15 million albums sold in just the past five years to determine their own direction on what would become *Desire Walks On*. First and foremost, Ann and Nancy Wilson were eager to get back to the business of writing their own material, with *Desire* producer Duane Baron recalling, "when we met with Ann and Nancy first in pre-production, first off, at that point they were tired of having people bring in the Diane Warrens and Mutt Langes and say, 'Okay, sing this, do that.' They were burnt out on that, and told us right out of the gate that they wanted to do a record that they wrote. It was more of a pressure for us, because in the back of our minds, we're thinking 'Okay . . .'"

> 'Ann and Nancy were just psyched to be writing their own record again.'

Longtime friend and co-writer Sue Ennis recalled, "On that album, we took the reins back in terms of writing. Ann and Nancy were just psyched to be writing their own record again. When we got back into the writing process, it was really fun, because an inspiration would just blow through, and you'd take the ride and see what happened. We decided to go a little harder with a few of the songs. We wrote them at Ann and Nance's get-away place at the beach, specifically the songs 'Desire Walks On' and 'Rage.' It just felt right, like, 'Let's see how hard and weird we can get in the title song,' and it was exhilarating to be writing like that again, because we knew John and Duane were rock guys. They had just come off a big Ozzy Osbourne album; I was personally a big fan of *No More Tears*. I also do think we were feeling some pressure from Denny, Mark and Howie to just rock it really hard. I remember us playing those beach demos for John and Duane, and they were a great audience to play those songs for, because it was like their wheels started moving instantly. Even before the songs were over, they were getting production ideas. Looking back, I do think the album got off track with too much tinkering, and it was a very, very expensive album to make. I mean, exorbitant. It took nine months or a year to make, and by the end, Ann and Nance were going, 'God, this album will never be done.' So they were just dragging themselves into the studio toward the end. Ultimately, it seemed to me that it was a little overwrought. In some ways, I'm still married to the original demos of the songs."

From guitarist Howard Leese's perspective, the shift was a double-edged sword, "I think the girls on that album wanted to get off the conveyor belt of making a record, going on tour, getting a two week break but having to fly somewhere and do a video. And the girls also felt a little misrepresented as artists at that point by not writing their own stuff. So they wanted to return to the '70s ethic, which made me a little nervous for obvious reasons." A decade earlier when Ann and Nancy Wilson — at the height of Heart's first commercial wave of success — had decided to swim against the current, it had cost them, and it took many years to make the climb back up.

One of the fruits of its commercial success was Heart's opportunity to construct their very own recording studio, Bad Animals. Nancy Wilson recalled, "When we built Studio X at Bad Animals in Seattle, it was the first world-class big room in town. The idea was to support the thriving Seattle music community plus our desire to work in our own hometown. Even though we ultimately took quite a loss on that investment, it's still used by all the Seattle greats, symphonies and other artists who need a break from the usual. It has one of the best drum rooms I've still ever heard, not to mention a beautiful spacious atmosphere. Good thing they haven't turned it into a Starbucks yet!"

The investment in the Bad Animals studio served as something of a safety net for producers Duane Baron and John Purdell, who had some trepidation about the uncharted waters they were heading into with recording *Desire Walks On* on the Wilson sisters' terms. As Baron recalled, "On that record, it was the Ann and Nancy show, so they had a vision and wanted to do it. They'd had their success, they had their money and were just tired of being, what they would kind of describe as being, a cover band, doing other people's songs. They wanted to make a record with their songs. Because they owned Bad Animals, their own studio in Seattle, we had the luxury of doing everything there." Ennis reflected, "I think they were excited about just having a state-of-the-art studio 10 minutes from their homes. They were happy to finally have a good studio in town where they didn't have to go off and rent houses in L.A., and drive in that traffic to Van Nuys every day for studio work. They had done that for so

> '. . . it was a really nice, luxurious time for us as artists.'

many albums, and having their own studio allowed them to make a world-class sounding record in Seattle."

The new studio represented both the capital and freedom the band had earned in the course of their seven-year rise back to the top of rock. Leese explained, "For that album, another big difference aside from using our own songs was that we built our own studio, Bad Animals, in Seattle, and that was the first record recorded there. I was a little involved in the design of the studio, I had a little input from a musician's standpoint, in that we wanted to have it so that everyone could be at their stations and see everybody else while we were playing, and so everyone could see the control room. So we had Ann on one side of the control booth in an iso-booth, and Nancy on the other side of the control room in an iso-booth with an acoustic guitar, me and the guys were in the main room, everybody could see everybody, and we could actually play live like we usually do. The studio's console was an ssl g-series. We'd hired the guy from Sweden who'd designed A&M Studios, because we'd worked there with Ritchie, and really thought it sounded good, and wanted something on par with that, which is reaching pretty high because it's one of the best studios in the world. So we spent a couple million bucks on that place, and the day we opened it, it was one of the state-of-the-art studios in the world. So in a way, it was a really nice, luxurious time for us as artists — we had a beautiful studio that was ours, and could pretty much take as long as we wanted and do what we wanted to do. So we just made sure to keep good self-discipline in a situation like that and keep our eye on the prize and do it."

The guitarist explained that the band was greatly aided in their effort to return to its 1970s rock roots by producers Baron and Purdell, who he felt "were a formidable team. Duane came from an engineering background, and John was a musician, so they had all the bases covered. He was a good keyboard player, could sing pretty good, and played some keyboard parts on the record here and there. Duane was a great engineer, and it was definitely a left turn production-wise from the previous guys in terms of the way Duane and John were working. They were happy to do the girls' songs, and make them as good as they could, and I don't think they were as single-oriented. They just wanted to make a good record for us. And everyone loved the new studio, so it was a little bit of a honeymoon — new producers, new studio, right in our hometown."

Ennis recalled, "My impression was that John Purdell was the more analytical and organized guy, who was really quick with technology, and made quick decisions. A forward-mover and big energy guy, as well as having a fantastic music theory background. Duane seemed like the soul of the team, more feel- and artistic-oriented, and maybe more of a rock kind of player. I just remember him being more about feel than analysis, but they made a wonderful team. Humor is the currency of the recording studio, and they were also very funny guys. I remember John being a little more buttoned up than Duane, maybe not quite as much of a big puppy. Duane would slouch into the couch and chat cheerfully, telling great stories. Very accessible, fun guy, and John was really nice too, but a little bit more withdrawn personally. They were wonderful to work with, always upbeat, and seemed very focused and organized about the recording craft. They were disciplined with planning the sessions in terms of exactly what would happen that day. In the same time, they were excited to experiment, and were collaborative and supportive with what Ann and Nance wanted to do. For instance, there's a song on the album called 'Voodoo Doll,' and they wanted to push that really far, so they had an African drumming group come in to add an extra instrumental track. I think Ann and

Nance felt really happy about the fact that we could take a demo, put it into the hands of these guys, who would take a simple-sounding demo, work on it overnight, and when we came back the next day, they'd have added a rhythm section, and say, 'This is the direction we're thinking of.' Ann and Nancy would usually say, 'God, that sounds great!'"

As unusual as it was for the band to be writing their own songs again, it was equally odd for Baron that Heart wrote as they recorded, a luxury that owning Bad Animals provided them. "*Desire Walks On* was probably the only record I've ever worked on where we did writing and pre-production while we were cutting tracks. We'd set up, the band would be there, and we'd start working on one song at a time. . . . Ann and Nancy both wrote the songs together — they're both totally deep into their music. We had these things we'd call kitchen parties where we'd go to Ann's place, and just listen to music 24/7. They listen to music non-stop, both of them. They get along so great, they're like twins, so they would sit there and talk together about song ideas, then write together. Nancy tended to come with more of the music, but Ann could also hear a melody and turn around and sing it to Nancy. They totally vibed off each other. I would say with them it was pretty evenly split."

On the band's seemingly enviable writing and recording routine, Leese reasoned, "Having as much time as we wanted was a double-edged sword because a deadline can be good. You don't want it to be where the work will suffer, but sometimes a time framework can be a good thing. To their credit, the girls had some good songs for *Desire Walks On*. We were fairly disciplined, we worked six days a week tracking, and when it came to mixing, we worked seven days a week. So it's not like we were lazy; we had it figured out pretty good. We did the bass and drums tracks over a five- or six-week period."

"Where with most records," described Baron, "after you've done your pre-production, it's like, 'Okay, we're going to set up the drums and cut the tracks.' And you cut all the basic tracks in two or three days, we had the luxury of the time in the studio, so it was actually fun. We changed some things with the drum micing, where I played around with room mics. That album was a good example of 'If you're gonna play around with drums, the thing you'll probably play around most with is room mics.' I think sometimes I'll just focus on room mics, but I'll keep my close mics there if I want to blend them in. But as far as playing with my placements, I probably play with that more than anything. I'll use old-school ways of just using the two-mic system on drums — the Glenn Johns approach — and set it up that way, but I'll always have in my back pocket the close mics. Thinking, okay, if this screws up, I can always go back to this or add this in, so I do play with things, but I always keep my mainstay. I have a pretty standard close set-up, but I like playing around. If it works great, good. Sometimes it does, sometimes it doesn't, but on that record, because of the way we were recording — writing as we went along — it would be like: we'd be writing a song, and someone would say, 'Let's try this on the drums,' where we room-miced only. Actually it was kind of cool, because we would spend maybe some songs one or two days on it, or on others, we'd spend a week. Because we'd be working on it, writing, listening to it in the control room, changing things around, so it gives you time to go, 'Let's try this on the drums, it might be cool.' Typically for drum micing, I like 421s on the toms, 57 on the snare, 441 underneath the snare, sometimes I use a 67 or 414 condenser on the floor tom, but usually I'll go dynamic for rock stuff. For the kick, I'll usually use a C-12 on the outer kick, because I'm a fan of using double-heads on kick drums. I don't like single heads, because I like the resonance it adds to the kick drum. I'm not a fan of tight, clicky kicks; I like the attack and feeling the kick decay after."

Leese noted, "Another difference with that record was our bassist, Mark Andes, had left, so we recorded the album as a

four-piece, and I played bass on some of the basic tracks, then would overdub guitars. When we started the overdubs, I'd come in in the morning, and do guitars during the day, then Ann would come in in the evening and do vocals, because she sang better in the evening. So we split it up that way, and that seemed to work pretty good. And even though our records in the '80s were sometimes called 'slick and too perfect,' they were all actually recorded in a very straightforward way, and were very live. The rhythm guitar was recorded live with the drums and bass, a lot of the lead vocal stayed, and those records are pretty live for how slick they sound; they're actually pretty raw. We were just precise players, so it sounds like we worked on every little thing and corrected things. Nowadays you can go in and fix anything — if you're flat, sharp, early, late, whatever, they can move it. We never did any of that stuff back then."

Baron agreed, "We tracked the band live where their instruments were in ISO-booths, Nancy and Howard, and Ann was playing bass when we tracked."

From a production vantage point, Baron explained, "Nancy, musically, is a great, great guitarist. With that record, I used pretty much my standard amp/mic set-up, because at the end of the day, I use the mics as crossovers, so there is no one set way — it will never sound exactly the same on each record. I've got so much control by using the multi-mic system, that I can whack a tone, and make it thicker, or brighter, so I guess the blend comes in each case based on what I'm hearing, or what the song should feel like, or what tone they're giving me. With Nancy, we always double-tracked her guitars, and on that record, Nancy did most of the rhythms. She wanted to do the majority of the rhythm guitar tracks on this album, so we did, and she did great. Sometimes she would get it on the first or second take; sometimes it took longer. I used a three-mic set-up usually, all 57s, where you have a mic directly on the center. . . . You have to understand the way a speaker works, I guess. If you were to mic just the center of a speaker, you're gonna get all top end. The further you get away from the center and go to the outer edge, you start to get mid-range. All your bottom-end comes from the outside of a speaker, your top end comes from the middle of the speaker. So if you just use one mic, say, on the middle of a speaker, all you're gonna get is a lot of top end, and it may sound good, but you're missing the bottom end that's coming from the outer part of the speaker. In other words, a mic can't really pick up a whole speaker on its own. But what you also have to keep in mind using multiple mics is that you have to keep the mics in faze, so what I like to do is keep the mic at a 45 degree angle on the outer cone, that's very important, and then put the mic in the center of the speaker for top end, along with the outer mic for bottom end. But keeping the outer mic at 45, keeping the capsules at the same distance from the speakers, again, for

> '. . . with most vocalists, you're trying to find a good line. With Ann, it was . . . "Which line was bad?"'

fazing. So what I do is use the mic like crossovers, and then I'll put a third mic at the middle of the speaker. So basically, I'm getting high-end, mid-range and low-end, and again I'm just using the mics as equalizers, as crossovers. So when I'm blending the mics, I get the full-speaker, which I think is really the key or trick to recording heavy guitars. Because there you're using the whole speaker, not just part of the speaker, because the whole speaker gives you tone. If it's in the middle, it's a thin tone, and it gets fatter with more bass as you go out. So if you're only going to mic one certain area of the speaker, well then I believe you're missing out on a lot of tone, and I think a lot of people don't know that."

When attention turned to the task of tracking Ann's now-legendary windpipes, Baron — as with everyone who had ever recorded her previously — found that "Ann was amazing to record vocally, the best singer I've ever worked with. The key with Ann was you hit play and record, and the song goes top to bottom. Then John and I would look at each other and go, 'Woah.' And then you'd do another track. We'd normally do three or four tracks and then do a comp. The thing about Ann was — normally when you do a comp with most vocalists, you're trying to find a good line. With Ann, it was backward, like, 'Which line was bad?' You're talking, going, 'They're all fucking good, oh my God.' It was a complete reverse from the way we normally did it. Most singers like to hear themselves wet when they're recording, but for pitch and stuff, most singers tend to want the reverbs and effects kept at a minimum. They like it in that there's a vibe there, so it's not like singing in a closet. Everybody sets up a little bit of reverb or delay, and most singers tend not to like to hear that while they're singing in the headphones. They kind of like it down a little bit. That was the case with Ann. Individually, Ann's greatest strength was vocally, no question."

Baron, not surprisingly, found the same to be true of recording Nancy. "They're amazing, and the fact that they're sisters also means they sound great together in harmonies. Because they were sisters, their tone — when they would blend together — was amazing. We didn't have to do any pitch correction or anything. In terms of Nancy singing leads, it was Ann who encouraged Nancy to sing leads. Nancy and Ann did their thing with divvying up harmonies. They tracked harmonies together on a couple songs, but for the most part, Ann would do her vocals, then Nancy would go in and do her harmonies afterward. I think Ann definitely has an easier time doing vocals than Nancy, but Nancy was great. There were no problems with either of them. They were psyched in general because we were doing a project that they wanted to do, not that other people wanted them to do, so I think they were a real strong team."

The only sore point during the course of recording *Desire Walks On* was the inclusion of the Mutt Lange–penned single "Will You Be There (In the Morning)" Contractually obligated to the pin-point extreme of Lange's approving the mix, which had to be followed note for note from the demo before it could be released, Baron recalled a potent tension. "When we were doing vocals, Ann would stop and go, 'I don't want to fucking do this, I've done this shit, I hate this.' So then it was John and I making the call on that, going, 'Okay, let's appease the label, let's do the song.' They didn't want outside songs, and again, the label was pushing, and we ended up having to do a Mutt Lange song, and Ann hated it. It was a total Capitol Records thing: they had signed a deal with Mutt to where if we were 'allowed' to do the Mutt Lange song, it had to be the first single, which none of us knew at the time we were cutting the song."

Adding further insult to injury, Baron explained, "None of us

'. . . we didn't know the deal had been signed already.'

liked the song, but we were ordered to do it by the label. That made it harder to produce, in that case, because it was a Mutt Lange song, so we had to constantly play him what we were doing over the phone. We had to copy his demo, and he had to hear it and okay it. He sent us the demo, and we had to mimic it — it was terrible. But the rest of the album was pretty much the girls doing what they wanted to do. I respect that. I knew where they were coming from and thought there were better songs on that album than the Mutt Lange song. But we had a saying in the studio with Ann and Nancy: 'in case of fire, we'll break glass.' In other words, if what we're doing fails, we've always got the Mutt Lange song in our pocket. Let's just do it, but in case of fire, we'll break glass and bury it on the album. But we didn't know the deal had been signed already at the label that it had to be the first single off the album, so we got kind of shanked on that one."

For his part, Leese explained, "I didn't mind it, because Mutt Lange wrote this, and the song had been recorded for Def Leppard. The demo sounded like a hit record, just like a Def Leppard single. He'd finished it a little bit too late to make the Leppard record, so he gave it to us, and it came with strings attached. I thought it was a real catchy, commercial song. It wasn't exactly what we did, and probably would have done better if Def Leppard had done it. But one thing that was hip about it was I had been suggesting for years that we sing in some other languages, so by the time we did that record I convinced John and Duane that we needed to do so, because there was all this huge market that we needed to break into. I had wanted Heart to do 'Alone' in Spanish for years; I thought it would have been a huge hit. So we had 'Will You Be There' done in Spanish, and next thing you know we're playing Chile, Mexico City, and suddenly a whole other half of the world opened up to us because we went and did a couple songs in Spanish. It wasn't our greatest single ever." Concurring, Baron concluded, "I personally really like that album, except for the Mutt Lange song."

In spite of the band's feelings, the lead single debuted Heart's eleventh studio album in the top 50 of the Billboard Top 200 Album Chart upon release in November 1993. Billboard praised the "catchy 'Back to Avalon' . . . Heart is enjoyable on Robert 'Mutt' Lange's power ballad 'Will You Be There (In the Morning),' the adult contemporary ballad 'The Woman in Me' and a cover of Bob Dylan's 'Ring Them Bells.'" Driven to platinum status by the singles "Will You Be There," "Black on Black II" and "The Woman in Me," Heart completed another successful world arena tour throughout 1994 before taking a hiatus from the grind of the machine that would last nearly a full decade.

CHAPTER 12

Heart's Hiatus and the Rise of the Lovemongers

1995–2001

For anyone familiar with Heart's love/hate relationship with mainstream commerciality, it came as no surprise that the band decided to take some well-earned time off as they headed into the mid-1990s. Ann Wilson told a journalist in 2001 that in light of the commercial success of 1993's *Desire Walks On*, "We thought, let's take a breather. Let's put Heart aside for a little while; not break it up, just let it breathe for a while. . . . That's why, at the end of the '80s, we decided to take a break from it — just put the old car up on blocks and work on it. We took a few deep breaths and decided how to present it fresh. That's why it's been so long since we had a studio album." Guitarist and co-producer Craig Bartock theorized that "because of the way both those girls are about those things, it's all about the spontaneity

'. . . they have no idea that she is nothing like that manufactured image.'

and the creation of the moment. That probably reeked havoc with them over the years, and certainly did in the '80s, and that's why they have such an unpleasant view of a lot of the producer-driven, Diane Warren–things that went against their natural instincts as artists."

Underscoring the latter point, Sue Ennis recalled, "It's funny because people have these images of sexy, pin-up Nance with big hair from those days. Sometimes I meet guys who say, 'Tell Nancy hello for me. I've had a crush on her since the '80s. She'll always be my first love.' Of course, they have no idea that she is nothing like that manufactured image. You would never find Nancy Wilson done up in a tart-like or come-on type of way. She's a down-to-earth, dog-loving, beachy girl, who wears jeans and practical large coats with huge pockets to carry dog treats and dog balls. She talked about feeling like she was being made-up for a play, back then, to the point where she was actually playing a role. For those of us who were around in the '80s, she would emerge from these make-up sessions with the big hair extensions and stuff, laughing in disbelief."

As a musical outlet during their vacation from the machine Heart had become — and as a way to keep in touch with the millions of new fans who had ridden along on the band's wild second wave of success — Ann and Nancy formed a side project, The Lovemongers. Nancy explained, "We were able to break loose of the '80s super pressures. We had just spent quite a few exhaustive years of extensive, massive touring, recording and making huge videos. It was an era of extreme overkill, which by the early '90s had seen the last of its big hair bombast. Then, when the Seattle sound came to the foreground, and it couldn't have happened at a better time for us, we were graciously welcomed back home to Seattle by the awesome new bands like Alice in Chains, Pearl Jam and Soundgarden. Finally, the culture began shifting back to something more authentic, more roots, so we took our new small, unmanaged, unsigned, un-imaged band back to clubs and played benefit shows. The joy came back to us because we were playing just for the love."

Years later, Ann Wilson told a journalist, "We put The Lovemongers together as a way of reconvening our original selves when we were kids. Just sing harmonies, it was all unplugged. I used to play bass, but other than that it was all unplugged. We just went out and played benefits and didn't make any money, didn't make any bucks at all. We just went out and played our favorite causes, went on tour, broke even or lost money. It wasn't a career thing at all . . . it was a thing for fun and rejuvenation. And from that came the idea of bringing Heart back, because we really missed the rock. Meanwhile, Nancy scored some movies with her husband Cameron [Crowe], I did some solo stuff, did some theater stuff, we had kids and we thought, yeah let's rock again, let's bring Heart back, it's time. That was 2001 and then we toured last summer and we're touring this summer as Heart with a new record."

Ann and Nancy Wilson's freedom from the pressures of Heart inspired longtime friend and co-writer Sue Ennis to join the band as a visible member for the first time in her more than 30-year history with the Wilson sisters. As Nancy recalled, "Sue finally joined up with us [along with another talented friend Frank Cox] in The Lovemongers in the '90s and it was like a best-friend dream come true for us. No managers, no record companies, no image-makers, just the love of singing and playing." Echoing Nancy, Sue Ennis recalled, "The group got together during the first Gulf War in the early 1990s, and the first show was actually at a Red Cross benefit for the troops in Seattle at the Paramount Theatre. Anyway, the Red Cross asked Ann and Nancy if they'd do an acoustic set, which of course they agreed

Nancy Wilson   Ann Wilson

THE ROAD HOME

to. I remember us all sitting around one night — Ann, Nance, myself and our dear friend Frankie Cox — after dinner, and the girls were saying, 'What sort of songs should we do? Should we try to skew any of the song choices toward the theme of the event?' So we sat around and

> 'No managers, no record companies, no image makers, just the love of singing and playing.'

started singing old Peter, Paul and Mary songs like 'The Great Mandela.' Frank and I were putting on harmonies over Ann and Nancy's leads, and pretty soon it sounded so good, that Ann and Nance said, 'You guys should back us up.' We had such a blast at that show that Ann and Nance said, 'This is what we need to be doing right now. Wouldn't it be fun to try and make a record?' So that's how it came about, a bunch of friends singing together. I believe the thinking was 'Let's surround ourselves with our beloved friends, making the music we love, and with no pressure and no middleman. Let's get back to the love of it.' Ann and Nance wanted to bring other people in to support their sound. So they really welcomed me as a third party and had even asked me to join their high school group at one point. But I wasn't cut out to be a performer. Being behind the scenes is more suited to my temperament. I would sing in front of them in the bedroom and put harmonies on together, but would never sing in public."

Ennis reflected that the side-group "was a reaction to touring with a demanding, sometimes whiny bunch of guys and then *Desire Walks On* was expensive, too much over-tinkering in the studio, many suits weighing in and breathing down Ann and Nance's necks. So The Lovemongers came along as sort of a sweet antidote to all of it. It was stripped down, acoustic all the way and back to the harmonies and roots of what had first gotten Ann and Nance excited about music. And they brought in

their best friends — Frankie Cox and me — as group members. We got a one-record deal with a little indie label here in Seattle called Will Records. So we wrote about 12 songs for the record. We did a lot of covers live to fill out our live show, and really only did one Heart song, which was a totally new arrangement of 'Crazy on You,' which was an idea Nance and I hatched as a showcase for Ann's voice. So we held a nice am7 synth chord, waiting for Ann to come into the song. 'We may still have time, we may get by . . .' As the song went on, she got to wail, baby. Going back to her bluesy Aretha Franklin roots. It was a showstopper and was our encore at our live shows. But the band was definitely a vacation from Heart, and was rejuvenating in a lot of ways. We made a Christmas album and I remember sitting in the studio with Daniel Mendez, our great engineer. The atmosphere was an upbeat and playful one, and Ann and Nance would often say, 'This is how you make a record!'" *Rolling Stone* reported at the time of the release that "the sisters are releasing *Heart Presents a Lovemongers' Christmas* on November 13th. A repackaging of their indie-label holiday album, the ten songs include three traditionals and seven originals, with titles like 'The Last Noel' and 'Bring a Torch.'"

While the majority of the touring Ann and Nancy Wilson did during the 1990s came via solo spots or with The Lovemongers, they did reunite officially as Heart for a live album in 1995. Entitled *The Road Home* with its cover featuring a childhood photo of young Ann and Nancy, the album was a celebration of the sisters' folk-acoustic roots, so much so that lifelong friend Sue Ennis explained that the album was reminiscent of "their high school group, The Viewpoints. That is such a big part of who Ann and Nancy are as sisters and musicians: musicality, vocal harmonies and that acoustic music." *Rolling Stone* praised the album's success in stripping "down the bombastic, arena-rock Heart of the '80s [revealing] its sweet folkie soul." *All Music Guide*, meanwhile, praised the band's live album, which featured hits "recast as intimate numbers; Heart manages to find new layers in all of these warhorses, partially due to the sublime production of [Led Zeppelin bassist] John Paul Jones. The result is Heart's best album in years — the old material sounds more alive than anything they have written in a decade."

Explaining how the band's vintage sound was captured live, engineer Brian Foraker began by recalling, "We had a different drummer and a different bass player, and John Paul Jones was a guest player on the album. We recorded it at a small club in Seattle, I cut it to digital, and rented every Neve module — 1081s and 1073s — on the west coast. It varied because there were only so many of them, but I wanted to make a warm-sounding

record. The coloration that they have, and a nice musical sound to them. And since I was using a digital tape machine, I wanted to try to get as much of that warmth as possible. One thing about digital that is still true today — whatever you put in is what comes out. So I was trying to get as much of it on the way in as possible. Working with John, who is a big analog fan, it just didn't make sense to bring

> '. . . it was such an intense and personal performance. . . . It's the most naked I've ever felt.'

in an analog console, because there were so many tracks. And I wanted everything individual for total control down the road. I also miced everything separately so I could blend things back to what was needed, not locking myself into anything. Because it was a club, and we had a recording truck there, but we just wanted it all under our control till we got it out of there. We recorded a couple shows, then went back and listened to both, and picked. 'Well, this song was better from this night, this one from that night.' I don't think there were any additional over-dubs, other than just replacing the strings on a couple of songs. We did that because live, it's hard for the strings to hear themselves, so we ended up replacing strings on two or three tracks. In terms of the live micing for the drums during recording, I used a 421 on the kick, a 57 on the snare, Shure SM-81s on the overheads. For the acoustic guitars, I ran them direct, which they needed to be for Live, but also used a Technica 441, which I would put on a stand in front of them while they played. And everything was double-recorded, just in case a mic got knocked over or something. Mixing was done in Seattle, on an SSL console at Heart's studio Bad Animals, and Ann and Nancy and John Paul Jones were also aboard for that process."

Not long thereafter, Nancy released a live album of her own — her first solo outing and first time in years on stage without sister Ann standing next to her. *Live at McCabe's Guitar Shop*, according to *Rolling Stone*, "was recorded before an audience of roughly 75 locals, admiring musicians and personal friends [witnessing] the grassroots recording of Wilson's solo debut at a neighborhood guitar store in Santa Monica, California. . . . Armed with just her guitar and mandolin, Wilson candidly and passionately performed a slew of her own songs alongside Heart classics and covers of songs by Paul Simon, Peter Gabriel and Joni Mitchell." *Live at McCabe's Guitar Shop* took Nancy back to her folk-roots, and the singer explained that "I used to do gigs like that a lot in college, but I prepared a long time for the McCabe's show because it was such an intense and personal performance. . . . It's the most naked I've ever felt, but I don't mind that."

Amazingly, according to sound engineer Brian Foraker, the album almost wasn't made, as "originally she just wanted to make sure it was captured on tape since it was her first time playing live on her own. It was the first time she'd played out live by herself, and she was living there while I was, and she wanted to play at a club called McCabe's. So somebody at the club recorded it off the console on DAT, and as I was getting ready to move to Nashville, I took her live tapes with me. I went through them on Pro Tools, and picked out and played with the best takes from nights one and two, like I had with the Heart record. And originally it was just a birthday present to her, but it turned into a record."

Around this same time, longtime Heart guitarist Howard Leese finally said goodbye to the group he'd helped discover and guide musically in the studio for more than 20 years. According to the guitarist, "When I left, there was really no big fight or anything. Nancy didn't really want to tour anymore. She had started a family, so there were a couple summers where Ann and I went out together as The Ann Wilson Band. It was a totally different band, we had some horns, and it was fine, but it wasn't Heart. So it didn't feel right to me. They weren't the same level of players I was used to working with, and we weren't playing all that much Heart stuff, and so the whole thing was getting a little bit softer.

It just didn't have the edge to it and the toughness to it, it was softer — musically, physically, and I just didn't feel it was that great. So we did those two little summers, and then the band split for good, and I went to play with Paul Rodgers. I've been with him since 1997."

Reflecting on the phenomenal success his band had achieved — twice — in the course of their 20-year career, Leese explained, "Looking back, I'm very proud of what we did. I think we were a strong band, and had a great, long run, and were huge there for quite a time. The '70s band was just this hippie band from the Pacific Northwest who got together and made a few great records; we were very lucky. The '80s band was a little bit more show business, but my personal preference — and you'll hear the opposite from the girls — I like the '80s band better. I thought we rocked harder and were tighter and bigger even as a smaller band. Mark, Denny and I were just a rockin' machine. We played well, everyone looked good, and we had all the bases covered with that band. I'm personally very proud of the '80s stuff, and think they're some of our best records."

When Nancy wasn't doing live acoustic gigs or touring with The Lovemongers, her primary musical focus in the 1990s was scoring the soundtracks to husband Cameron Crowe's block-buster films like *Jerry Maguire* and *Almost Famous*. Recalling the genesis of their creative collaboration, Nancy explained, "When Cameron was working on *Say Anything*, he asked me to sit in for his scoring artist Anne Dudley for some guitar parts. I was so nervous to walk into a studio where the musicians actually had *charts* on their music stands. Intimidating. When I became the main scoring artist, I learned much more about myself as a writer and a player. It's usually a far cry from songwriting to instrumentally support the emotional arc of a scene while attempting to disappear at the same time. That quest for deceptive simplicity comes in very handy while scoring."

Heart guitarist and co-producer Craig Bartock noted, "If you

> '**Looking back, I'm very proud of what we did. We were a strong band.**'

listen to what Nancy does with her husband's movie scores, you'll hear a lot of organic *Oh Brother, Where Art Thou?* type of homey string things, and it's not always just an acoustic guitar with a capo. Nancy's always the first one to pull out a ukulele or a dulcimer, or a mandolin, or mandocello, or whatever instrument she happens to have at her disposal, and try it. So when Nancy does a score for Cameron, she's the first one to pick up a bizarre instrument and create a mood. She's got a good ear when it comes to grabbing a stringed instrument that may not be an electric or acoustic guitar, and finding a part for it."

On Nancy and her husband's creative chemistry, Ennis offered, "I think that as a team, their friendship and spiritual connection all started over a passion for music. When he writes a script, he's always listening to music, trying to figure out what songs will work. He really has a pretty clear idea of what the instrumental cues should sound like. He gives her his thoughts and she goes off and delivers something better than he'd imagined. He has said Nancy is his favorite acoustic guitar player, and so I think he gives her some direction for the cues he's looking for, but she knows just what to give him because their relationship and friendship really informs the creative process."

Nancy explained the specifics of her writing process, "Because I am lucky enough to know the script quite well beforehand, I usually start building the music cues, as they're called, ahead of time. In many cases those pieces fit perfectly into a scene later. Only a little music editing would be necessary. My music editor, Carl Kaller, is such a wonder when it comes to taking pieces and moving things around to fit the picture, even as the picture keeps moving and changing around till the last minute some times. We have worked together on movies now for 10 years and it's becoming ESP! When I do play to picture, it's always a challenge to time it all out, and perform like you're not thinking about the time limit. But I think the main gift of scoring is bringing the personality of the characters to light. Each main character should have his or her own melody or type of theme and style. In songwriting, it's usually more personal, especially when you also have lyrics to think about. I could never choose one above the other though. Songs are hard to write and score is hard to write, and once in a while, when something goes right, it's equally exciting!"

Spending years with Heart out of the recording studio rejuvenated Ann and Nancy's creative spirits, and exorcised many of the demons they had battled throughout the 1980s. The freedom the Wilson sisters had explored for the seven years apart from Heart eventually led them back home to a band that had a quarter-century under its belt as hard rock's only female-fronted living legend. Feeling it was time to start anew with the new millennium, Heart's beat soon began to pick up pace as they moved toward the full-fledged revival fans had been waiting the better part of a decade for — back to the live concert stage, and most importantly, back to the studio.

CHAPTER 13

Jupiter's Darling

2002–2004

By the fall of 2001, Heart had been on hiatus from the studio for the better part of eight years. While Ann and Nancy Wilson had reached fans' ears via solo tours and a live LP respectively, Nancy had relocated to L.A. to start a family with film director husband Cameron Crowe, while sister Ann had stayed in Seattle. In October 2001, it would be long-time journalistic friend *Rolling Stone* who would officially announce, "Ann and Nancy Wilson are ready to begin recording again as Heart." With their twelfth studio LP, Heart decided to return to its '70s style, which had defined the band as one of hard rock's greatest.

The creative impetus behind the band's new sound originated largely with Nancy, who explained, "on the most recent Heart album, *Jupiter's Darling*, I worked on every aspect of the

> '**There was no rock star/music producer dynamic, rather it was two old souls meeting.**'

writing more than I'd ever done before. I started working with a new collaborator, Craig Bartock." Bartock, who would go on to fill the now empty spot of Heart's full-time lead guitarist, recalled that his collaboration with Nancy began more than a year later in the spring of 2003 due to "Heart and I sharing the same management, and I got a call saying Heart was considering starting their first new album in thirteen years, and would I be up for writing with Nancy. And that was a no-brainer, so I said yes, but Nancy and I had never met prior to this. So she had no idea whether I was a guitar player, but she knew I was a songwriter and music producer, and somebody thought we would click. So when Nancy came over to my studio, there was an instant bond, because we share the same love of The Beatles and Led Zeppelin, were roughly the same age — so there was literally half a degree of separation between Nancy and I. It was just an instant bond, to where I think we both felt like we should have known about each other a long time before, but were just meeting. There was no rock star/music producer dynamic, rather it was like two old souls meeting and hanging out. So that first day, we ended up writing three songs, two of which ended up on the album. Nancy is very prolific as a writer, she has a lot to say.

"It just clicked so much that Nancy and I found a way to get together as often as possible, and this was before their '03 tour, so this was the first couple of months in that year. So she would come to my studio two or three times a week, right in the center of Hollywood, right on Sunset, and everything would click every single time. I would just set up a mic and let it run, and the ideas would come so fast, that for like an hour and a half, two hours, I would let the tape run, then go back and re-absorb what we had gone through. It was amazing. Our routine was we'd sit across from each other, and she'd usually have an acoustic guitar, and I'd have an acoustic or sometimes an electric guitar, and we'd just bat around ideas. A lot of times I would have templates ready for her, where I would say, 'Hey Nancy, what do you think about this chorus idea, or this hook?' So I would run a lot of ideas past her. She would come over, and these wouldn't be long writing sessions, we'd get together for an hour, hour and a half, and write two or three songs. I remember one really, really interesting thing, where Nancy — in order to kick-start herself for lyrics — brought in this huge, huge notebook she told me she'd had since college. And it was filled with hundreds of pages of poems, and written words, and she would leaf through it for inspiration. And she left it at the studio once or twice, and I remember just opening it up and leafing through it, and I was just blown away by how prolific she was. Nothing was dated, so I don't know whether she did it when she was 16 or 35 — but I just thumbed through it thinking, 'Wow, this is a woman who really has something to say.'"

As the duo immersed itself even more into songwriting, Bartock explained that Ann inevitably rounded out the process. "When we were writing with Ann, at first Nancy and I writing so much was just a logistical thing, since Ann lives in Seattle, and Nancy and I both live in L.A. So what happened was Nancy and I would write the songs, then she would e-mail MP3s to Ann, and I think as soon as Ann realized there was something pretty special going on in the songs we were writing, she flew down and the three of us got together. I sense she felt really good there was something organic and real happening, because they had fought the '80s thing so much in terms of just being producer-driven. That had caused them to take a break in the first place. So the chemistry she saw first between Nancy and I, and that developed quickly between Ann and I and the three of us, made everybody recognize we were trying to do something real here. We were

trying to take Heart back to the '70s, glossing over the huge production and drum machines and synthesizers and reverbs and
multi-track vocals, and trying to pitch everything. Instead the
writing was speaking more to us saying, 'Okay, it's time for Heart
to make a legitimate, real record with real songs that Ann and
Nancy wrote,' and Ann recognized that. So probably a month
and a half into Nancy and I writing together, she came down and
joined us in that process, and it was amazing."

Nancy herself recalled that the album truly began to take shape
when "Ann came in as a writer." Explaining the process by which
the trio went about crafting *Jupiter's Darling* thereafter, Bartock
noted, "One of the great things about both Ann and Nancy is they
have amazing filters. They're very smart people, but they can filter
things very well. So they have a way of listening to a raw piece of
music, like a snippet of a chorus or a melody line, and instantly
saying, 'You know something, that's what we need to work on,' or
'That doesn't feel like us.' They're both brilliant at that. So I would
run a lot of ideas past Nancy, and then we'd find ones that seemed
to make sense to work on, and just literally flesh it out. Nancy
wrote the majority of the lyrics on *Jupiter's Darling*. Ann and I
probably wrote two songs together, Nancy and Ann and I wrote a
couple songs together, and then the rest — everything except for
'Lost Angel' and 'Down the Nile,' both of which were two original
songs they'd written before we met — Nancy and I had written
together. It seemed to happen so fast." Nancy was so impressed
with the writing chemistry the three had that she asked him to
produce the album with her.

Bartock shared the details of how they put together demos of
the new material, "When Nancy and I first met and were doing
this, I would try to capture the energy of the writing session ultimately, and Nancy certainly doesn't need to sit around and
watch me come up with drum loops and bass parts. So what
would happen is, she would take off, then the next day when she
would come back, I would play her the demo of the song, and a

lot of times she would make suggestions, or put more guitars on it. Or we'd speed it up or slow it down, or change the pitch, then she would sing the demo. Then we'd send them off to Ann. Our routine was to have a songwriting day, where Nancy and I would spend a couple of hours writing. And it would be fast and furious, because we would be like two 13-year-old kids with guitars, sitting in a garage writing, and it would be like the first time we'd ever written anything. We were just bouncing ideas off each other! So by the end of those couple hours, we'd have a pretty good idea of what the verse, chorus and the bridge would be like. So then after she and/or Ann left, I would physically put a demo together, and the demos didn't sound a whole lot different from what *Jupiter's Darling* turned out to be."

With writing for the album going so well, the Wilsons decided to continue with it even as they were on tour, taking advantage of the advent of portable digital recording technology. Bartock explained, "Pre-production actually lasted throughout their tour in 2003, because throughout the spring Nancy, I and Ann had been writing at my studio. Then when the summer came, they took off to go on the road, and they had already worked in four songs I'd written with Nancy into their live show to see how they flew with the audience. I think the songs were 'Oldest Story,' 'Lost Angel' and 'Move On,' and so I wanted that process to keep going while they were on tour. It seemed a shame to have everything stop for those three months they'd be gone, so what I ended up doing was just continuing my work building the songs we'd written, and I'd e-mail MP3s to wherever Nancy was on tour. So after each show, when she'd get up to her hotel room, she could log on and she'd get a new song idea from me, then in a lot of cases, I'd get these wonderful phone calls at two in the morning. She had a way of calling me when she'd just got done playing and into the room, and didn't realize it was two in the morning, and she'd scream into my phone, 'BARTOCK!' I'd be dead asleep, and she'd scream my name, and I knew it was Nancy, and I also knew she'd liked what I'd sent her. So some of the album's final cuts turned out to be a product of writing via e-mail, songs like 'I Need the Rain,' 'Love to One' and 'Hello Moon Glow,' at least four or five songs."

Coming off tour in the fall of 2003, Heart dove headlong into completing pre-production for the album, drawing on the audience's reactions to new material they had worked into the band's live sets. "We reshaped some songs a little bit based on the audience reaction while they were on the road that summer," explained Bartock. "For instance, 'Lost Angel' originally had this huge, long opus in the middle. There's a section in 'Lost Angel' which has a guitar solo and string arrangement that was three times longer on the original demo. It had much more of a 'Mistral Wind'–type of hugeness to it. It's still very epic, but the original version was probably closer to nine minutes, where it clocks out at about six minutes on the album. I remember doing a lot of orchestration: tympanis, a lot of cellos, in case they wanted to go there, I wanted to be prepared. They were constructed with a lot of samples, at the time back then I was using EMU sampler. Also there was a lot of Mellotron, because Ann, Nancy and I all loved the way The Beatles used the Mellotron, and Led Zeppelin."

For Bartock, *Jupiter's Darling* was "probably the best project I've ever been involved with, just in terms of chemistry with Ann and Nancy. As reflected by the time amount to actually do it, it's a huge album in scope. It's 16 songs, and we recorded more that didn't make the CD. So the thing I'm proudest about is where it all started, and just how we got to say what we wanted to say. In the early 1990s, Heart got tired of being told where to stand and what kind of hair to have and what to sing, they rebelled against that, said, 'Okay, we've had enough of this for a while, let's raise families.' Nancy said, 'I'm gonna help Cameron do his movies, and be behind him,' and Ann said, 'I need a break.' They did The Lovemongers thing, and just needed a break from the largeness of it, like an avalanche. And it took all those years for them to go, 'You know what, we just want to be ourselves. We don't want to spend too much doing one song, and sit there listening to some producer go through snare drum sounds for a week.' It's so easy to get bogged down in the minutia of that, so when I came to work with them, we all knew the bottom line that no one had improved on those original Chuck Berry records. There's a magic there that no amount of re-writing verses, Pro Tools magic, or no matter how many plug-ins you stick on, or how many reverbs you try, at the end of the day that doesn't mean a thing. So I think the ultimate lesson that can be learned with *Jupiter's Darling* is finally let Ann and Nancy be themselves."

Recording got underway, Bartock recalled, "in my studio, because I had pre-demoed all but one song on the album, so we had a very good template going in to do the album. It was already done on Pro Tools, so we had very good sketches of all the songs. In my home demo studio, I had a Mackie digital board A/B, and Pro Tools 5.13, and in order to create more of a live feel of what I thought Heart should go for in terms of drums, I would take drums from previous project sessions, and time-stretch them, and edit them in Naked Drums. So I would just edit and time-stretch the drums through that software, and end up with much more real feel than the '80s, quantized Lynn drum–type sound. So the demos had real drums, because I sensed from a lot of conversations with Ann and Nancy during our writing sessions that they were going for that '70s sound. They were not fond of the '80s, and made that clear, and so we were all going for bringing Heart back to when they were a real band. So even in the demos, I wanted everything to be kind of sloppy, not quantized, with kind of a 'Stonesy' feel. Having everything pre-produced and green-lighted before we ever went into the studio with Ben and Mike, and just sitting in front of a console going, 'Okay, now we're making a record.' It just made things so much easier, because there's nothing worse than five people sitting around a studio staring at each other when the clock's ticking. There was none of that. In fact, when we recorded the proper album, it went quickly, where I think we recorded the whole thing in six weeks.

"We recorded it on an SL digital console, and there wasn't an enormous amount of time spent working on parts, it was more about Nancy going out there and playing what was right. You're gonna find with a player like Nancy who's a seasoned guitar player, she's going to instinctively play the right thing. Years of experience growing up in bars and playing songs teach you this is the right thing for the song. And those girls know what's right. We didn't want to get bogged down in the technical aspect, or just nitpick over every note. We all knew how to play our instruments. The thing ultimately to remember about Ann and Nancy, and I don't think they had an opportunity to do this in past albums with past producers, is they have a real good sense of what's right: the right part to play. Then we took a little break, and Nancy came back in and did all her guitar overdubs." For the album's vintage '70s drum sound, Bartock described an at-times experimental set-up in which "there are some songs where we actually used a cardboard box for a kick drum, which we miced with an RA-20, which we also used for the regular kick drum, and a Shure SM-57 for the top of the snare drum, and Senheiser mics for the toms. We actually used six sets of overheads. We had overheads for the drums, and then a couple more ambient mics probably 10 feet away, then we put another couple ambient mics probably on the other side of the room, just in case we wanted to go for the John Bonham thing, we had the option. As far as the specific mics, I like to use 414s a lot for overheads, KM-84s, and definitely a lot of Neumann mics."

On the new album, Heart was also going for a guitar sound that Ann Wilson told *Rolling Stone* at the time "rock[s] . . . so much harder [than our last album]. . . . The new album is going to be really loud!" In detailing the treasure-trove of gear the trio used to turn the volume back up, Bartock began with amplifiers, musing, "I don't think we used the same amp on the same guitar twice, and I don't think we used any new amplifiers. Everything was all analog, vintage tube amps; Nancy is a huge analog person. She is all about putting the dirt back in, the warmth, she wants to see the tubes glowing! As a matter of fact, instead of using a digital slap delay, she brought in an old two-track reel-to-reel she had as a kid, since the '70s, to use a slap delay, and it sounded amazing. Amplifier-wise, I had a tendency of using Vox amplifiers; I'm a Vox fanatic, which ultimately comes from The Beatles connection. The Beatles used Vox amps, and they have yet to make a better amplifier. They're not always ideal for live use because they're a little temperamental and they don't have master volumes on them. So in order to get the best sound on a Vox amp, you just have to turn it all the way up and stand back. It's only a 30-watt amplifier. I had four AC-30s from the early '60s, I had my AC-10, I had a couple of solid-state Vox amplifiers. There were times when we were using old Sears amplifiers, anything that we thought would create the vibe. There wasn't any sense of 'Oh, it has to be a Marshall.' A lot of times, they would be smaller amplifiers — late '50s, early '60s models, and a couple times, Nancy used my AC-10. As far as mics, we used a lot of SM-57s, and a lot of times we would have a couple of microphones positioned for ambience. A lot of times there'd be like two SM-57s, one in front of the amplifier, and one behind the amplifier, right inside behind the speaker to get the 'oomph' side of the amp. But we probably had 30 of them laying around, so whenever we'd go in to do a song, we'd audition them, and pick the amplifiers we felt would create the vibe we were trying to ultimately achieve. There were pods used occasionally, but mostly it was all amps and older microphones, and a lot of tube compression, and that's how we got our sound."

Moving onto the guitars, Bartock recalled, "As far as electrics, Nancy is a Les Paul girl, and she's a Tele girl. Those are the two guitars she will grab for the most. She also has an old SG standard — very much like what Pete Townsend used, red with two humbuckers — and a very old Les Paul I believe she acquired when Cameron was doing *Almost Famous*. She used that quite a bit on the album. Those were her go-to guitars. My rig included an early '70s Sunburst Strat, which I find seems to work in a lot of occasions, and I have a limited edition '71 Les Paul with P-90s, which is basically a copy of the '55 Les Paul. And I would always watch very carefully to what Nancy was using: if she was using a Les Paul, I would use a Strat. If I saw her pick up a Tele, a lot of times I'd use a Les Paul, so that if she was going for the bright sort of Telecaster sound, I'd pick up a Les Paul and go for the fatter sound. So there would always be two sides of the coin when it came to electric guitars. As far as acoustic guitars, she had a couple of old Ovations; she was the Ovation poster girl back in the 1970s. She really helped put that company on the map, and it's owned by the same company that makes Takamines, and we used a lot of Takamine guitars. We also used a couple of Martin acoustics."

The Wilson sisters so channeled their Beatles' influence on the album that, according to Bartock, "right away when we started the recording process for *Jupiter's Darling* in Seattle, Ann and Nancy brought these guitars into the studio with them. They were replicas of the three well-known guitars that John, Paul and George used at the height of Beatlemania . . . a black Rickenbacker, an Hofner Beatle bass and a Gretsch Country Gentleman. They had made these non-working guitars when they were little girls with bits and pieces of wood and scraps lying around the house. They were done with great detail . . . fishing line for the strings, etcetera. We propped them up there in the studio so they could watch the goings-on for the next month. I remember thinking that they were the true symbol of why we were doing this: two girls with such a love of music that they just had to make copies of their idols' guitars. It wasn't about the money or the fame, but for the love of it and because they had to. It's like there was a bigger calling. The job chose them, not the other way around. In the end, it's all about the love for those girls!"

In describing some of her preferences concerning guitars, Nancy Wilson told a journalist, "I'm excited to have a relationship with Epiphone too. You know, my whole thing has always been about vintage guitars. That's all I've really played for the past 10 years, so when you guys sent me a guitar on the road I was kind of like ok, I'll try it. I mean, Epiphone has a rich history and, like Gibson, has been around forever, so why not try it? But, when I plugged it into my set-up, it was . . . wow! This is really fun to play! It sounds great! That Epiphone made me feel like Jimmy Page or something. . . . Then when I got the prototype of the Les Paul Ultra I took it into the studio and was able to find that certain type of distortion that I'm always looking for . . . and is hard to find. The one where there's enough 'clean' in it that if you want to play open strings like an acoustic . . . like the way Neil Young's distortion often sounds. It's beautiful enough to pull off any style of playing, not just big rock block chords, you know? You can play open strings or acoustic type figures and the distortion doesn't cancel the open strings out. The Ultra brought that to me. I think it's partially due to the open spaces inside the body. . . . [The chambers] make the guitar lighter but also give it a new sound you don't get with a solid body, a semi-hollow body or a hollow body. So, I'm really loving that guitar a lot! . . . And in the studio I've noticed the sound is a little richer because of the slightly acoustic tone. It's not enough that it's really different. I can still get that heavy, fat-rockin' sound but even when I play it acoustically in the room there's a little more you can hear. It just shines without even plugging it in . . . which is cool for a quote 'solid body.'"

From a fellow guitar player's point of view, Bartock commented, "I found Nancy's approach to guitar sounds in general was a gritty, 'Stonesy,' over-driven bluesy guitar tone. She has a tendency of liking those sounds, kind of a Keith Richards approach, where she likes it to be dirty and bluesy, and is really comfortable with that. She's truly one of the best rhythm guitar players in the history of guitar. It suits her well, because she's not a light guitar player; she digs in as hard as any guy you can imagine when she gets on a guitar. She's got vice grips for hands — she can *play*. She can sit there and strum and hit those strings as hard as Pete Townsend, and with that in mind, she likes to feel the air being pushed out of the amplifiers. It's almost an American-blues gritty type of sound, so knowing that head-

'She's got vice grips for hands — she can *play*.'

ing into recording, I went the opposite direction, more toward the British, mid-rangy, Beatles-esque, Brian May–Cream sort of guitar tone for myself. I knew that would instantly accentuate Nancy, and when we play live to this day, it's very representative of *Jupiter's Darling*. She would have this tendency of using the rhythm pick-up on a guitar, and getting that sort of chunky, bluesy sound, while I would use the treble pick-up, and get more of the mid-range, Cream-y distortion. So when you think about it, we were filling in each other's gaps."

Besides just guitar playing, Bartock also discovered during the course of recording that Nancy "is the queen of the stringed instruments, and we dug out a lot of instruments. For instance, if you listen to the intro of 'Make Me,' Nancy had an acoustic guitar made for her just for that intro. It was a Takamine acoustic with some kind of fancy tuner put on the low E-string, so that she could tune the guitar with a tuner, have it stop at a drop D, and then she could tune it back up to a standard pitch. You can hear her doing that at the start of the album. Nancy also used these three very old mandolins, each are over 100 years old, Gibson mandolins. She has the entire family: the regular man-dolin, the medium one and a third called the mandocello. It's a huge mandolin you can play bass notes on. It almost sounds like a mariachi bass. I believe that's Nancy playing the bass notes on 'I Need the Rain' on her mandocello, which just had an amazing sound. The wood's been sitting around for 100 years soaking up all this wonderful smog and atmosphere and music we had. She had an old pump-organ which I played on 'Hello Moonglow' and 'I Need the Rain,' so Nancy would have no shortage of

stringed instruments. She played auto-harp and an old dulcimer on 'I Give Up,' and she had a thing called a Marxophone. This was an interesting instrument from the turn of the century, sort of like an auto-harp, but instead of pressing the keys down, you strum. So you press the key down and it has a little hammer that strikes, and it sounds almost a little bit of a cross between a harpsichord and an autoharp. She'd always say, 'I got this really weird instrument laying around, I don't really know what it is. . . .' But she'd bring it in and make it work. She's got a way with all stringed instruments, in just finding the right part for it. It wouldn't take long, she'd go out and doodle for a few minutes, then go, 'Okay I'm ready, record me.' It was pretty brilliant."

Another of Bartock's favorite moments recording Nancy came "when we were recording 'Oldest Story in the World,' if you notice the way it starts out with a feedback guitar. How that came about was when we were recording it, during lunch, we spent a lot of time watching The Beatles' *Anthology* on TV. So we were watching when they were talking about recording 'I Feel Fine,' and Paul was recalling how when John had leaned his acoustic Gibson guitar up against the amplifier, it started feeding back. And The Beatles had said, 'Wow, what an interesting idea!' So I turned to Ann and Nancy, and said, 'You know something, interestingly enough, we have that exact same box amplifier and acoustic Gibson guitar sitting in the studio right now.' So we went out after lunch, and re-created that feedback from 'I Feel Fine,' and that's what you hear at the beginning of 'Oldest Story.' We used a couple of old Telefunken mics, a couple of tube Neumann microphones, and on the amp, The Beatles were using a Vox AC-100, and we had a Vox AC-30. So we set it up, and Nancy just leaned the guitar up against the amplifier then turned up the volume, and we did about four or five takes until we got one that was really close, then edited it onto the beginning of the song."

Yet another of the producer's favorite products of *Jupiter's Darling* came with "I Need the Rain," which "was the only song that was recorded differently than everything else. Originally, this was just an interlude, and when it came time to actually work on the song, Nancy and I were sitting in the studio, and she said, 'You know, this is too good to be just a 20-second interlude. This needs to be a song.' So she and I sat there before everyone came into the studio, and just wrote the whole song in the control room, lyrics and all. Then Nancy and I went out into the studio, separated by a glass booth, and Nancy had her mandolin and I had a Papoose guitar, which is a half-scale, tuned up to a fifth, and is a cross between a ukulele and an acoustic guitar. It's very chimey, pretty and bright sounding, so once we found a tempo and got a click, we faced each other, and recorded the mandolin and acoustic guitar together for the whole song. Then a couple of hours later when the band showed up, they overdubbed bass and guitars to what Nancy and I had already done, and then Ann and Nancy added vocals."

Prior to any vocal recording session beginning, Nancy recalled, "we took the luxury of singing 'hootenanny' songs to warm up

> ‘We would have a hootenanny every single day . . . to help Ann warm her voice up.’

first with Craig Bartock.” Elaborating further, the producer explained, “When Ann started coming in for vocals, which would usually be about twelve or one in the afternoon, we had a specific idea where the three of us would sit around — it was already set up like a campfire — and we would have microphones on us, and three acoustic guitars. And we would have a hootenanny every single day, and it was Nancy's idea to help Ann warm her voice up. And fortunately, not only would it warm Ann's voice up, but it would also put us in this wonderful mood to sing, and that had a lot to do with my bedside manner. So after Ann singing for an hour and a half of just her favorite songs — from The Beatles to The Beach Boys to Neil Young, to Motown and Neil Campbell — where there would be a lot of funny moments, like ‘Oh My God, do you remember this song?’ And we'd break into that, and it just set this wonderful tone. It wasn't technician/producer–singer, it was just three people sharing an amazing love of music. They actually recorded all those hootenannies, so somewhere someone's got probably 30 hours of Ann, Nancy and I singing every song known to man.

“Then after a while, I'd go, ‘Ann, are you ready?’ And whenever she was ready, I had already set up a Sony or a lot of old Neumann tube U67 microphones, and the best way to describe Ann Wilson's singing technique is she's like a Ferrari. She goes from zero to a hundred in about three seconds, where once we got her engine warmed up, and when she was ready, we stuck her in front of that microphone and you just let the track go. What I found fascinating about Ann is it's kind of like data transfer, where you get it so fast. Once her voice is locked up, you go maybe four or five passes, and go, ‘Okay Ann, I think we've got what we need, but we can always re-approach it tomorrow if we don't.' And I would usually go into the studio the next morning before Ann and Nancy showed up, and would listen to what we'd done the previous day, and the day we were doing it, I didn't understand the brilliance of what Ann was doing till the next day. Because once I'd stepped away from it, I remember listening to the vocal and going 'Holy crap.' There wasn't a lot of nitpicking, and Ann really shines as a live lead vocalist, so we tried to capture the band feeling of what it would have been like to be back in the '70s. And to not get so hung up, like for instance they do sometimes in the R&B world, where you hear about Michael Jackson having 48 vocal tracks. Honestly, even if there was something that was pitchy, but Ann believes it, I'll take that anytime over a technically perfect vocal. Ann has perfect pitch anyway, so it was all about emotion: do we believe what she is singing? So she just went in and hammered those out. I remember it being a wonderful, symbiotic relationship where we just got her in this wonderful mood, threw her on the mic and just stepped on the gas, and she would take off."

Turning from Ann to Nancy, Bartock further explained, "Vocally, Nancy had a very different approach than Ann did. Ann was a bit of a Ferrari, where Nancy was much more analytical about her vocals. For the songs like 'I Need the Rain' and 'Hello Moon Glow,' the songs she sang on the album, Nancy would have the tendency of being a bit more critical. She would do the vocal, come in and listen to it, and go, 'Ah, I can do that better,' and go back out and do it again. And she was always right, but by the same token, she didn't spend a lot of time either. Though where Ann would say, 'You know something, you guys are producers, I trust you guys. Let me hear it when it's done and it's sitting in the mix, and I'll let you know if there's anything I want to re-do.' Nancy would have much more of a 'Let me go out there and fix this one line. Let me see if I can do that better.' Still, it didn't take a whole lot longer than Ann, because those girls can really sing. I have sat between Ann and Nancy many a time in the studio and live, and I hear them very loudly in my ears, and they don't hit a sour note. They're that good. Nancy's voice is stunning, and in any other band, she would be the lead singer, she just happens to have Ann Wilson as a sister."

The song on the album that Nancy was proudest of was "'Lost Angel,' which I penned alone; [it] really hit the spot I was aiming for. It was written when the war in Iraq was about to engage and I think the whole world may have been feeling a lot like that song." Bartock, for his part, cited "The Perfect Goodbye" as being among his favorites from the final 16-track listing, reasoning "it's probably the most accessible song on the album. I remember Nancy was leaving after a writing session in my studio one day, and she said, 'Oh, you know something, I have this great idea for a song, it's a Cameron line called "The Perfect Goodbye."' Cameron is the king of coming up with those lines; he's a genius when it comes to that. And she said she was thinking of making a blues song out of it and left. Well, the next day when she came back, I had written the chorus idea, and a basic sketch for the verse. And I said, 'Nancy, you cannot use "The Perfect Goodbye" for a blues song; this has hit written all over it.' And she said, 'Yeah, let's go for it.'"

Nancy also cited "big favorites of mine [as] . . . ones Ann wrote on her own like 'Sweet Darling' and 'Angels.' 'Angels' still kills me with that awesome and deep simplicity. Sometimes the hardest thing to pull off is apparent simplicity." Speaking in broader terms, Bartock felt "what we accomplished ultimately with *Jupiter's Darling* is they said what they wanted to say. If you read into that album, they're saying, 'I hate the '80s, I hate drum machines, I hate synthesizers.' There are no synthesizers on that record. 'We like guitars, we like good honest rock 'n' roll, we like songs that say something.' For instance, Ann even got a chance to do some spoken word, if you listen to 'Down the Nile,' there's a huge section at the end where we set up a microphone and said, 'Ann, say whatever it is you want to say.' And she's talking, none of it was scripted, and she said whatever she wanted to say.

That's the first take on the record, and that's the brilliance of Ann Wilson. She can disarm somebody or praise them quicker than anybody I've ever seen. I ended up using a thing called an Ebo, and I put it on a bass guitar, ran it through a Vox box directly into the board. And I started doing all these weird, snakey bass guitar things on this Ebo while Ann was out there doing this rant/spoken word thing. It's just a reflection of us saying to them you say whatever you want to say on this album."

Eager fans and critics alike seemed to agree with the direction Ann and Nancy Wilson had decided to return the band to musically. The new album came full-circle, and *Rolling Stone* drew particular attention to it in terms of its "production — by Nancy and guitarist Craig Bartock" as foundationally important to providing "Ann's voice the powerhouse space it deserves." The magazine further celebrated the pleasure and treasure of "hearing the sisters truly doing it for themselves." Ultimately, in Bartock's opinion, what he, Ann and Nancy achieved on the band's twelfth studio LP was responsible for "the chemistry of what's happening with Heart in 2008, I think it started with *Jupiter's Darling*. It had to do with 'Okay, it doesn't have to be epic, it has to feel right.' And this translates to the way this band is today. I was just out to dinner last night with Ann, and all the guys in the band, the crew, we're family. Whenever we haven't seen each other for a few weeks, Nancy has this thing she does where she laughs sarcastically and says, 'Ha ha, my band!' We hang with each other, and care for each other, and it's one of the important reasons why we still tour every year. We really feel we've come full circle, and we enjoy going out, with Ann and Nancy making comments to me that this is the best Heart that has ever been. And we're still hungry for the right reasons, and I think this band is edgier than ever before because we're doing it for the right reasons finally."

CHAPTER 14

Hope & Glory

2006–2007

In 2006, Ann Wilson began working on a solo LP of cover songs, following in sister Nancy's earlier footsteps on *Live at McCabe's Guitar Shop*. Conceptually, *Hope & Glory* was best explained by *Billboard Magazine*'s review of the LP: "Ann turns her attention toward songs that ostensibly deal with social and political hot-button issues, loaded with messages of war, peace, hard times and, mostly, imminent doom. It's a bleak album to be sure, undoubtedly inspired by the downtrodden national mood of the times in which it was recorded (that would be the George W. Bush era — perhaps it's no coincidence that the album's release date fell on the sixth anniversary of 9/11)."

Commenting on what inspired her thematically in the course of plotting *Hope & Glory*, Ann Wilson told one journalist, "I'm a total peacenik. I think we should be out of the war. It's a complete disaster. It's really upsetting. Another thing that bothers me is dogfighting because I'm such an animal person. Dogfighting represents the worst side of human nature. It drives me insane." Still, Ann's motivation wasn't entirely political in her song selection for the LP, explaining in the same interview that "each of these songs holds a special place in my soul. . . . At one time or another every one of them has kept me up at night to the point of exasperation and will not be banished, as I lay sleepless on my pillow. Such songs as these carry me through my life, and they are a standard to which all new music I hear and write must compare."

Heart guitarist Craig Bartock, speaking on the band's behalf, felt that "it made sense for Ann to limit her involvement with any of the members of Heart, aside from Nancy, because she wanted it to be her own thing." To that end, the album contained only one song penned by Ann Wilson, "Little Problems/Little Lies," whose inspiration, the singer explained, stemmed from the conceptual theme of the album, "We decided to write from the very first day, but it took me a really long time to figure out who I was and what my lyrics could be inside this album. But then I thought, 'Why don't I be a soldier in Iraq lying down to die, bewildered, and summing things up.' I wanted to keep it simple and use the language someone would use at a time like that. When we first started working on the album, some people were like 'Do we dare take some sort of global, political stand?' Because generally there's music and there's this other thing way over there — politics. But it's become so pervasive, it's all fused together now, so I don't think anyone has to worry. . . . I'm not a real prolific writer. I don't write songs all the time. I maybe write half a dozen songs a year, tops. ['Little Problems, Little Lies'] was the best of the best as we were working on this record. I put it last on the record because it's meant to tie everything together. It's the only song on there that relates to the world right now. I had the idea from the beginning, but it took me a long time to

figure out what voice to put it in. . . . I believe this is good music for people to hear, to help to contemplate our world now."

Ann once again enlisted the help of sister Nancy, as well as lifelong friend Sue Ennis, in the course of choosing a track listing comprised of classics the trio had grown up listening to. As Ennis recalled, "Before she went in to record it, Ann made lists of songs she loved that had some kind of pertinent social message, that was what she was looking for. I think I threw a bunch of ideas her way, and one night we brainstormed together." Wilson, for her own part, explained, "I just didn't want to haul out and make a solo album. . . . I wanted to wait for the right idea, the right producer." When Wilson had her track listing finalized, her quest to find the right producer eventually led to longtime k.d. lang producer Ben Mink, who recalled the gig came his way after "I got a call from John Varant from Rounder Records, Ann's label, and had previously spoken to Ann and Nancy about *Jupiter's Darling* a few years prior. At the time I was producing with k.d. lang, and so we put it on the back burner, and then got a call about Ann's solo LP. The concept was already formed by the time I got in the picture, and I think really came from Ann wanting to do a record of covers. To be honest, I really would have loved to have done a record of original material. But there were enough great songs that addressed the issue that we felt we could say what we needed to say.

"I'd never worked with Ann before, and wanted to try a couple songs, and see if there was chemistry, what her ideas are and who she is as a person, because you're going to be spending a lot of time with this person. So she flew up to Vancouver from Seattle and we spent a couple days in the studio, and about 25 percent of it was great, and another 25 percent could have been great if she'd had more time, but I liked her as a person. I liked what she said, she's incredibly intelligent and very, very funny, and I figured, 'Okay, if I'm going to spend a bunch of time making a record with someone, this is a person I can enjoy the time with.'"

While it eventually became an album of duets, Mink explained that at the outset, "as soon as I said, 'Okay, let's try this project,' the guest-star idea came about. I got an e-mail from her manager Carol Peters saying, 'We need some guests. Elton John has consented to do it,' and I realized this was going to be in a completely different realm than I'd imagined. I thought it was going to be a boutique, west coast, kind of little rock record, but it became this complete other thing that really spoke volumes about the scope of Ann's influence across the board. Both as a writer and as an unprecedented, great rock singer, because she's a prototype in many ways, she is. There's the Janis Joplins, but there's not a female rock singer on earth that doesn't have something she owes to Ann, I don't believe anyway. There is nobody that sounds like her — when she lets it go, it's absolutely astounding to sit there and listen to that. So the legends of the people I was working with definitely weighed enormously on me during recording.

"We had about a week to a week-and-a-half of basic tracking, where we used one drummer and rhythm section, which we recorded up in Seattle. We tracked 16 songs, and then picked the ones we felt were the strongest at the core so it had a band kind of sound. After that was done, some of the tracks worked and some didn't where I completely discarded the drums, and re-interpreted it completely." When attention turned to Ann's legendary lead vocals, the producer explained that in spite of that legend, "that didn't mean she was perfect, it really depended on the song. Where Ann had trouble, it really depended on her mood. Like all great singers, she's enormously influenced by her mood. You have to learn how she best feels relaxed, because she was going through an enormous amount of personal change with her mother dying. We had days where we got good results out of that, and then days where it was just impossible for her to sing."

When Ann was tracking, Mink found himself most impressed by "her timing — the pocket is incredible, which I guess comes from years and years of playing with rock bands with great drummers, but you either have it or you don't. In the studio, she's a great improviser; she has the most amazing way of casually tossing off a line, like one of those little 'Yeahs,' or 'Oh yeahs.' Just the tiny things that somehow force the ear to listen to

it. Also, she has better phrasing than I think almost any singer I've worked with. It's amazing." To capture Wilson's storied voice, the producer explained that "as far as mics, I used a number of different things, in my studio I used a PLM and 103, and we used a U47 and a U67 in the studio on Ann. Generally with Ann, it was a U47, and the chain was usually an 11-76. I'm really not that particular, I run through a bunch of them. I'm very much about performance, and so if it's a quiet song, sometimes I'll try a mic that will have the singer practically kiss it. You can make a microphone sound like 10 others dependant on your proximity, and then EQ's another situation entirely. So I don't stress about that, because when I'm tracking it's all about performance. There's always a way to tweak something and make it work, but we mostly used the great traditional mics on Ann's voice — U47s, U67s and Neumanns."

For overdubs and mixing, Mink described, "I tend to throw a lot down and see what sticks, because much like decorating a house, you have one object in the center — for instance Ann being the painting on the wall — you have to know what furniture to bring in, and you have to know what to take out. There's many ways to approach it, but to me it's like building a house, a lot of it's architecture: how you frame the voice, if the wrong instrumentation doesn't work. So I used one basic rhythm section then took it home and puttered around a lot just to see what would stick. And some things didn't need much work at all, and others were works in progress till the very last mix day. Elton John's song was one example of that, where we were still working on the vocals till practically mix day, and the arrangement, the beginning — just getting that to grasp into the rest of the song was a big problem. And 'Little Lies' waited till the end, and you often don't know what's missing from a mix until you're there, and you realize, 'Oh God, this could really use another electric.' And you'll do that, the vocals will be done, and you'll put one more on, and it will end up being the central instrumental part. I added one more electric guitar on 'We Gotta Get Out of This Place,' and it was at the very end, and it really helped glue it together. And not a small part either. As far as how much Ann hung around the studio for mixing, there were some songs she wanted to be there for at an earlier stage, but we generally would get the mix as far as we thought was the best, and MP3 her. She'd open it up in the e-mail, make some more points, we'd make changes, MP3 it again and live with it overnight. Then she'd come in and we'd listen to it on the big Superscope speakers, and if there was something to change, or if she wanted to change a line

— occasionally she'd fix a line or add a little harmony. But we just do that quickly, and that was the mix. She was definitely not standing on our necks at all, it's a lot of trust, and I take it as a real compliment. Because it can be a nightmare sometimes when an artist makes one song into a lifetime project during mixing, you can spend your whole life remixing something, and there's a time to let go. And Ann was great that way, she didn't waste any time."

In citing some of what he felt were Ann's strongest and smoothest vocal performances, Mink begins with Led Zeppelin's "Immigrant Song," explaining that it "was the very first thing we tried together, and I think I used about a third of what she sang that day on the final track, but when we did overdubs and tracked the drums, she sang a couple more times. But that song was pretty natural for her, vocally. In terms of songs she nailed and I didn't have to touch a thing, 'Isolation' was one example where she did three takes and I think I used two lines from the second or third, but it was basically the first take as is, didn't have to touch a thing. She came back from the funeral, and it was no surprise to her, because it had been a long, painful process of her mother dying. So from the time her mother finally let go, I think it was two days later she tracked 'Isolation.' She came in like a real champion, she's a very strong woman, and just stood up there, and I knew what was going on with her, and just quietly prompted the other guys in the band not to expect anything because she was in a lot of pain. And she just stood up there and opened her mouth and sang it. It's one of those time when you listen to it going down and just know provided the engineer has done his job and pressed record, there's nothing more to do."

While most of Ann's lead vocal tracks were recorded in Vancouver, Mink revealed, "None of the guest stars came there to record." Beginning with he and Ann's recording of their collaboration with Elton John, the producer recalled, "We went down to Vegas to do Elton's session. He had a certain amount of time to do the track, and we had done a quick demo for him without piano, just a quick sketch. So we went to Caesar's Palace at a show he was playing, and did it with some remote equipment on stage. So it was just myself, Ann and Elton in the afternoon at Caesar's Palace, with the lights dimmed, and a sea of red seats. And Ann and I were sitting in the front row with headphones on, sitting waiting for Elton, and it was as surreal a moment as I'd ever had. So when he came out, he was completely professional, and even took the role of session guy, instead of Elton John, and it was his own song. But it had been so many years since he'd played it, so he had a lyric sheet, and had to go over the piano chords the night before. He was so considerate and accommodating, asking me, 'Is that piano take alright, do you need anything more?' They used an old classic Neumann on his voice, and he did a warm-up, then one or two takes, and said, 'Do you think you have enough for what you need?' And it was a completely different interpretation from the original, because his voice has changed a lot over 30 years. So he had to reinvent his own melody to make it work, and it was just fascinating to watch his mind work, because you see how prolific he is and how quick he is, and exacting."

Continuing with what most impressed him about Elton John during the course of recording "Where to Now St. Peter?" Mink excitedly explained, "He has such a forward motion, and there was a clique track he was playing to, and he was consistently on, slightly ahead, definitely in a leadership, forefront role in his own song. Because he has such a strong intent — that's what really impressed me, his intent and energy was palpable, it really was when he played. He gave so much, it was not like a rehearsal. When he sang, he threw his hands up in the sky like he was praying, he really gives. He had a rough vocal of Ann's he was singing to, but he brought the whole energy level up so high on the track that we went back and completely re-tracked her vocal. Elton's words at the end of his vocal session was 'You're going to heavy it up, aren't you?' So we added drums and bass with Heart's

> 'Elton was hearing the song . . . as much more powerful and angry.'

rhythm section, and then Ann, once we had Elton's vocal, had a chance to approach it as if she did it live. We didn't really rehearse anything, I just stuck her on a mic and said, 'Okay, pretend he's here and sing.' And she did some just amazing stuff, sang amazingly well."

Sharing her own memories of the song's recording, Ann explained to a journalist, "I have always loved this Elton John/Bernie Taupin song. I'm a *Tumbleweed Connection* addict — that's my ultimate Elton John album. When we went to Las Vegas to record Elton for the song, he required a chart because he hadn't really thought much about the song for 30 years. Soon Elton was hearing the song in a different way — as a much more powerful and angry song. So he put down his piano and his vocal, and I had to go back and record my vocal because he had gone up like four clicks. Elton was so giving and so strong on this version. He got up after doing his 'The Red Piano' show the night before, played tennis, took a shower and then reported to duty for me. Thank you, Elton."

Turning to other stellar collaborations on the album, Mink begins with Ann's duet with the producer's longtime creative partner k.d. lang on "Jackson." "Ann and k.d. were there together in the studio when k.d. sang on 'Jackson,' which we did up in Seattle, but Ann's vocal was already tracked. k.d. was always a big fan of Ann's, and always used to sing Heart songs in her bedroom as a teenager, so when I mentioned I was going to be working with her, she was totally up for it." Wilson recalled of lang that "I found her really charming. . . . Of course, she and Ben Mink are like an old married couple. He draws her out. . . . Some people heard the title and figured that I was doing the June Carter/Johnny Cash duet. It will be a fine surprise when they realize this is actually a great Lucinda Williams song from her *Car Wheels on a Gravel Road* album. I'm such a fan of Lucinda's and everything she does. I just think she's one of the finest writers of this particular time. I especially love how deceptively simple her lyrics are and how blue she can get. Damn, the woman just can get so far down and it's so beautiful the way she takes us with her."

Of Ann's collaboration with Winona Judd on both "We Gotta Get Out of This Place" and "Get Together," the producer recalled, "They didn't sing live, but both were there the whole time. When Winona was sitting there doing her vocals in the room, as it was going down I'd make comments, and when I had the mute button on so Winona couldn't hear it, I'd ask Ann, 'Well, what do you think of this, what do you think of that?' And she has great instincts, she really does, but it was very open and friendly. She'd either give me her suggestions, or we'd leave the mic on and both talk to Winona directly. I think Winona and Ann, when they got wailing, you really almost lost track of who was who." Ann commented that with "We Gotta Get Out of This Place," "I was looking for a song that would relate to the whole idea of just busting out of this negative cycle we're in these days. It's my way of saying, 'Let's just get out of this damned repeating cycle.' When I thought about doing a song in those terms, 'We Got to Get Out of This Place' came to mind. In that context, the line 'My little girl you're so young and pretty' was to me a mother speaking to her daughter. Maybe they're both stuck in some backwater place and the mother is old before her years and the daughter is on her way. Of course, she's a single mother — the stereotype . . . just like me. Wynonna and I — our paths have crossed a few times and we just hit it off. We're two of a kind. I thought of her and Naomi and their history and figured it would be so cool to do this song with her, especially if she starts it out because she has that whole deep Elvis Presley, Mae West–y thing going on in her voice. With 'Get Together,' we realized that doing

HOPE & GLORY   *249*

this Youngbloods smash — written by Dino Valenti — could be inviting scrutiny because it's sort of the ultimate hippie anthem with its whole peace-and-love type message. So it could have been a real *Spinal Tap* moment, but then we decided we love the song so let's just take a moment and figure out how we can do it for now. And when Nancy started singing on it, it just became this beautiful new thing and we thought that 'Yeah, this works.' Why not? It's still a very beautiful musical statement, and there ought to be room for that even now."

As for his experience recording a pair of singers who shared a track as well as a last name, Gretchen and Ann Wilson, on "Bad Moon Rising," Mink recalled, "Ann already had a pretty good vocal down, and Gretchen came in — Nashville style — right on time, 'Let's do it,' and sang an excellent harmony. Her instincts were great too, but it occurred to me that they were both sitting there and fans of each other, and said, 'Look, the ending has that party kind of vibe, why don't you both go out and see what happens with two mics.' So of course, as soon as they were there, I said, 'Why don't we just run from the top,' and instantly it became another thing — so much different. There's something that certainly becomes three-dimensional when there's two people feeding off each other. The energy is very different, like acting with someone on film versus live on stage, and because they were both right there, the final take was live." For her own part, Ann felt that Gretchen "is powerful and she has her head screwed on, a great voice and she wants to rock. She can really sing country, but deep inside, there's a rocker trying to get out. . . . We did the great song John Fogerty wrote for Creedence with Gretchen Wilson. Recently Gretchen stood up with Alice In Chains at the VH1 Rock Honors and sang 'Barracuda' and was awesome, really awesome. Gretchen wants so much to be a rock singer and I think she's shown that she can do it all. The song itself is on the fence between rock and country — it's very swamp rock like Creedence could do sometimes.

I thought Gretchen brought a lot to the track. She's very pure and it was great of her to find the time for us."

Ann's favorite collaboration, of course, came with her sister Nancy, which Mink recalled was "amazing to watch — an 'Everly sister' thing kind of happens. Because they can practically look at each other's eyebrows, and know that if an eyebrow raises, then the other one's going to sing higher. So then the other sister will intuitively go lower, and create the right harmony. It's a lifetime of that for them, so it's second nature. But their voices do blend in that genetic way that only siblings can blend; it's a natural double-track practically. But their voices individually are completely different. Their version of 'Everybody Get Together' went very quickly. Nancy was there, and it was just a joy to work with Nancy; I'd never met her before. But we just sat down and started playing guitars, and we have very, very similar sensibilities when it comes to strumming and backgrounds. And there was really nothing to talk about, I just picked up one of her instruments she'd brought along, a mandola, and we just faced each other, she played guitar and played it, and it was so natural. Then she and Ann stepped up to the microphone, and I would say in two-and-a-half hours the track was basically done."

While many of Wilson's critics pondered in their reviews why Ann didn't pursue a full-fledged solo LP of originals, Heart insiders speculated that her choice was a simple reflection of Ann's feeling more comfortable performing original material written with sister Nancy alongside her — be it in the studio or on stage. Ann herself admitted in one interview that "I am used to working with Nancy. . . . It's an artistic friendship that has been going a long time and is really empowering. . . . I just don't understand what it's like to be all on me. . . . I'm not used to saying, 'I,' because it's always been 'we.' So doing this solo album has been a really big experience for me. . . . She told me, 'Whatever you want me to do, I'm there.' . . . Everyone around us was like, 'Make sure no one confuses this with Heart,' but Nance

and I never have any hesitation to be there for one another."
Hope & Glory producer Mink qualified the latter by recalling,
"Ann's solo record in many ways was her first record, because
she's so used to being there with Nancy. There was a long lead-
up time to Ann getting into a comfort zone, and when we finally
got to Los Angeles, and it was the first time Nancy was there, it's
the first time I'd met Nancy, but Ann was so much more relaxed.
For instance, when we did 'Darkness, Darkness,' I was playing
electric live with Nancy, and Ann was singing, so that was a live
trio thing. And as soon as that happened, and Ann's headphones
were full of that guitar interplay, distortion on one side, distortion on the other, she just wailed. It was the first time I heard her
really jive, there was no thought behind it, she just purely
emoted. It was fantastic, she came back out, sat down on the
couch quiet, and she was home. It was where she liked to be: next
to Nancy. They really love each other; it's so lovely to see how
much they care about each other."

Still, in spite of the historical precedent that Heart had cast
— in both the personal and musical context of Ann and Nancy
together — the *San Francisco Chronicle* remarked in its review,
"the album comes alive because Wilson allows herself to slip out
of her comfort zone." Either way, critics broadly received Ann's
gift with open ears and hearts, clearly in consensus on a point
that *USA Today* made best: "this batch of socially conscious
covers (plus one original) — the sentimental 'Little Problems,
Little Lies' — finds the Heart siren sounding a different alarm."
That alarm, according to *All Music Guide*, is "Ann's voice . . .
strong and convincing" on what the *San Francisco Chronicle*
concluded was "a high-minded concept album that takes its
inspiration from our bleak political times. . . . Wilson reinter-
prets their anxious visions to comment on the current
geopolitical malaise." Wilson's hometown paper, the *Seattle
Times*, further noted that "[Wilson] is still one of the best female
rock singers, her voice pitch-perfect and crystal clear as she rock-

ets from throaty growl to piercing howl. . . . Wilson's command of hard rock set the standard for a generation of female singers." But arguably the critics Ann enjoyed hearing from most were her friends and family, beginning with sister Nancy's conclusion that "Ann's solo album has my wildly enthusiastic two thumbs up!" Sue Ennis concurred, declaring, "I really love the album. I think it's carefully and lovingly crafted. It's artful." Heart guitarist Craig Bartock felt that *Hope & Glory* was "a brilliant album, it's a very consistent, tight album, she picked the right songs and it flows very well. I think they did all the right things with that record, I really do."

2008 and Beyond

Not many bands have a legacy that includes more than 30 million records sold worldwide, twenty Top 40 hit singles, and four Grammy nominations. Generation after generation of Heart's fans have shared in their love for a band that the *Los Angeles Times* called "so singular . . . [that] we forget how many women have really made an impact on mainstream rock . . . hard rock, you can almost count them on one hand." *Rolling Stone* recently praised Ann's vocal prowess, "For a vocalist to be wowing us 30 years after we first heard her, is something. . . . There is no one better than Ann Wilson." Because Heart insisted on opening eyes, ears, minds and hearts with their music, Ann and Nancy Wilson are already part of the annals of rock history, not only as songwriters and artists but as pioneers for women in the male-dominated music industry, paving the way for up-and-coming female musicians to be taken seriously for their work.

While those people closest to Ann and Nancy feel the best is yet to come, such as Heart guitarist and co-producer Craig Bartock, they share the opinion with critics that "there's no doubt that Ann will be remembered as one of the greatest female vocalists of this entire rock generation, and she continues to write the book. It becomes even more obvious when we do these shows like 'Decades and Crossroads,' and we have other people sit with Ann and cover our songs, and you realize there's really only one Ann Wilson. She sings everything in the same key she sang 30 years ago; her voice is like a fine wine. The great thing about it is you can uncork it, and take a sip out of it anytime you want and put it back, and it keeps getting better and better. I don't even think she's reached her stride yet." Lifelong friend and collaborator Sue Ennis, meanwhile, offered her insight into how the Wilson sisters might like to be considered in rock history: "I think they would want to be remembered for their songwriting and their musicianship. Ann's got a gift that has been both her salvation and her burden, and I think she would be proud to say she was known as a great singer. I think Nancy would feel the same way about her guitar playing and her songwriting and her amazing harmony ability."

Underscoring just how groundbreaking a rock 'n' roll band fronted by two women was in the 1970s when Heart was first hitting the scene, Mike Flicker, producer of their early albums, recalled, "When I produced *Dreamboat Annie*, the whole album, [Heart] didn't have a record deal in the U.S., and when we first tried to get them signed to a label, we got almost the same thing from every label, from every A&R man: 'Well, are they a rock band, a pop band, or are they an acoustic band?' That album was all of those things. 'We can't sell that.' A girl rock 'n' roll band is a great idea, but that's not what they were, and I think what happened was Heart was at the forefront of opening up the gate to: you don't have to be pigeonholed. Especially being females, they got it worse, but you don't just need to be one genre, which was the norm at the time. And I think Heart opened up a lot of opportunities for a lot of females in rock by doing a multi-platform crossover at radio with that album."

Looking to the future, Ann and Nancy continue to keep the

musical beat of their creative heart alive and flourishing, not only through their bond with fans, but with each other. The secret to Ann and Nancy's sustained success, as their mother Lou once told *Rolling Stone*: "The girls have been able to hold onto the friendships and the values they've had from childhood. I was so afraid when I saw they were intent on entering the world of show business. But they haven't gotten tough or hard. . . . It's a miracle. . . . I don't have all the answers to why they haven't changed, but I have a theory." According to current Heart guitarist and *Jupiter's Darling* co-producer Craig Bartock, the answer lies in the fact that "they are not only very close sisters, but they're soul mates. In real life, they're the Lennon/McCartney that didn't break up in 1970, and they still have that connection."

Offering a recent example of the Wilson sisters ongoing creative connection, Ben Mink, producer of *Hope & Glory*, recalled that during the making of that album, "it was interesting to watch Nancy when she was singing a harmony on 'Darkness, Darkness' from Ann's solo LP. Nancy's used to taking that secondary role. I just asked her to try a couple of impromptu things, and she would sing off-mic. She would sing turning her head to the left as if Ann was there. So she's used to that secondary supportive role, and we talked about it and she laughed because she knew it was probably true. They're a great combination, one of the great ones." As Ann told a journalist in 2007, "I don't think we ever clash . . . [because] we love each other so much. Nancy is my best friend. And she would say that I'm her best friend."

After 30 years writing songs together, the Wilsons have more than mastered their craft as Sue Ennis can attest. "Just recently, in September 2007, Nance and I wrote a new song together for the Seattle Children's Theatre. (Ann wasn't available.) I hadn't written with Nance in a good long time but it was just this incredibly high, thrilling experience to write this song. It was almost effortless. The shorthand we'd developed but hadn't really touched in a long time was still there, and we just had conversation back and forth, with guitars. I'm proud of that song actually because it proved that the creative avenue is still open for us. It was a pleasure to be at a place in our song craft where we've both achieved a certain level of expertise. It's an instinct of knowing how to structure something, knowing what works and what's lame for a song. The long road of writing all those songs has led to a certain ability where we really know how to write a song."

While many of Heart's contemporaries are content to tour the nostalgia circuit playing their old catalog, Ann and Nancy prefer to reward their fans' longtime loyalty by populating their live set with hits (often with reworked arrangements), an impressive range of cover tunes and new material. In that spirit, throughout 2007 and the spring of 2008, they have been plotting their thirteenth studio LP of original material. Nancy explained that she, directionally, "came up with a concept for the new Heart album recently and so far we've had only a little time to jam on it as a band. It is definitely a concept album in the classic sense, but I really don't want to give too much away just yet. . . . Ann and I have been writing together." Ann provided a few more clues to a journalist late in 2007: "We're just getting going on the new album right now. It's still very formative. Nancy has a big idea for it to be a concept album having to do with our family, our parents and our story."

Elaborating further on what the Wilsons have in mind as they write and record their next studio LP, Bartock explained in late 2007 that "Nancy came to me in the spring of this year and said, 'You know, what I'd really like to do for the next record is kind of a Pink Floyd approach.' And all of a sudden I was kind of like a dog when someone walks in the room with bacon. And many discussions have come from that about making an album like *Dark Side of the Moon*. Ultimately, we can't help but have songs that are accessible, because we all came through the same filter of loving The Beatles, the Stones and Led Zeppelin, all of whom write songs that have choruses. The ultimate thing is let's just make an album that says everything we want to say, politically — and let's not worry about Clear Channel, radio play . . . Let's just make an album that says what we want to say. We kind of got together at a studio in L.A. in June of 2007, and as a band we all sat around and just recorded jam sessions. Then we took the best bits and put it together on a CD and lived with it. In the meantime, I've put together about 10 song ideas in my home studio, sent them to Ann and Nancy and asked if any are jumping-off points for new song ideas. It's all been really positive feedback. I think the Heart legacy is still being written, and *Jupiter's Darling* played a huge part in that, and the next album will do that too."

For more than 30 years, in the studio or on the concert stage, Ann and Nancy Wilson's lives and music have blended as naturally as their legendary sibling harmonies. In the eyes of lifelong friend Sue Ennis, this is simply because "so much of what Heart's music is, is who Ann and Nancy are. It very much defines their music." Intentionally or otherwise, Heart began a revolution for women in music more than three decades ago, breaking genre barriers and garnering popular and critical acclaim. Even the Wilson sisters have a hard time selecting one element from their unique blend of music, as Nancy concluded: "It's impossible to name one favorite Heart album, though a combination of two or three might work. If you mix parts of *Little Queen* with a dash of *Dog and Butterfly* and sprinkled in some *Jupiter's Darling*, you'd have a nice gourmet meal of Heart music prepared, of course, with love."

Discography

1976–2008

Dreamboat Annie

1976

Singles: "Crazy on You," "Magic Man," "Dreamboat Annie," "(Love Me Like Music) I'll Be Your Song"

Little Queen

1977

Singles: "Barracuda," "Little Queen," "Kick it Out," "Love Alive"

Magazine

1978

Singles: "Heartless," "Magazine," "Without You"

Dog and Butterfly

1978

Singles: "Straight On," "Dog and Butterfly"

Bebe Le Strange

1980

Singles: "Even it Up," "Bebe Le Strange," "Break," "Raised on You," "Sweet Darlin'"

Greatest Hits Live

1980

Singles: "Tell it Like it Is," "Unchained Melody"
Note: Nine tracks recorded in studio, nine recorded live

Private Audition

1982

Singles: "This Man Is Mine," "City's Burning," "Bright Light Girl," "The Situation"

Passionworks

1983

Singles: "How Can I Refuse?," "Sleep Alone," "Allies"

Heart

1985

Singles: "What About Love," "Never," "These Dreams," "Nothin' at All," "If Looks Could Kill"

Bad Animals

1987

Singles: "Alone," "Who Will You Run To," "There's the Girl," "I Want You So Bad," "Wait for an Answer"

Brigade

1990

Singles: "All I Wanna Do (Is Make Love to You)," "Wild Child," "Tall, Dark Handsome Stranger," "I Didn't Want to Need You," "Stranded," "Secret"

Rock the House Live!

1991

Singles: "You're the Voice"

Note: Recorded live on November 28, 1990, in Worcester, Massachusetts

Desire Walks On

1993

Singles: "Black on Black II," "Will You Be There (In the Morning)," "Back to Avalon," "The Woman in Me"

The Road Home

1995

Singles: "Alone" acoustic, "The Road Home"

Note: Live album of acoustic/unplugged material

These Dreams: Heart's Greatest Hits

1997

Note: Greatest hits collection released by Capitol Records

Greatest Hits

1998

Single: "Strong, Strong Wind"

Note: Collection of hits from 1976 to 1983

Greatest Hits: 1985-1995

2000

Heart Presents: A Lovemongers' Christmas

2001

Note: A holiday album first released in 1998 as The Lovemongers, and re-released in 2001 as Heart

The Essential Heart

2002

Note: Two-disc greatest hits collection spanning 1976 to 1995

Alive in Seattle

2003

Note: Two-disc live album

Jupiter's Darling

2004

Singles: "The Perfect Goodbye," "The Oldest Story in the World," "Make Me"

Love Alive

2005

Note: Greatest hits collection featuring songs recorded between 1977 and 1983

Love Songs

2006

Note: Collection of Heart's greatest love songs

The Lovemongers

The Battle of Evermore (1993)

Whirlygig (1997)

A Lovemongers' Christmas (1998)

Nancy Wilson

Live at McCabe's Guitar Shop (1999)

Ann Wilson

Hope & Glory (2007)

Nashville-based music biographer Jake Brown has had seventeen books published, via multiple publishers in countries including the U.S., Europe, and Japan, on subjects including rock legends like Heart (authorized), Mötley Crüe (authorized), the Red Hot Chili Peppers, late funk legend Rick James (authorized), as well as a variety of hip-hop artists, including Biggie Smalls, 50 Cent, Jay Z, R. Kelly, 2Pac (authorized via the estate), Death Row Records CEO Suge Knight, the Black Eyed Peas, Dr. Dre, Kanye West and others. Brown's titles have received press coverage in national publications including MTV.com, *Vibe*, *Publishers Weekly*, *Ebony*, *The Source*, *Jet*, *Black Issues*, *Metal Edge*, and the Fuse Television Network as a featured biographer, among many others. Lastly, Brown is also founder/president of hard rock record label Versailles Records, distributed nationally by Big Daddy/MVD Music Distribution, since 2001.